A QUILT·BLOCK·CHALLENGE
Vintage Revisited

Mary W. Kerr

4880 Lower Valley Road · Atglen, Pennsylvania 19310

Schiffer Books are available at special discounts for bulk purchases for sales promotions or premiums. Special editions, including personalized covers, corporate imprints, and excerpts can be created in large quantities for special needs. For more information contact the publisher:

Published by Schiffer Publishing Ltd.
4880 Lower Valley Road
Atglen, PA 19310
Phone: (610) 593-1777; Fax: (610) 593-2002
E-mail: Info@schifferbooks.com

For the largest selection of fine reference books on this and related subjects, please visit our web site at www.schifferbooks.com
We are always looking for people to write books on new and related subjects. If you have an idea for a book please contact us at the above address.

This book may be purchased from the publisher.
Include $5.00 for shipping.
Please try your bookstore first.
You may write for a free catalog.

In Europe, Schiffer books are distributed by
Bushwood Books
6 Marksbury Ave.
Kew Gardens
Surrey TW9 4JF England
Phone: 44 (0) 20 8392 8585; Fax: 44 (0) 20 8392 9876
E-mail: info@bushwoodbooks.co.uk
Website: www.bushwoodbooks.co.uk

◆ ◆

Library of Congress Control Number: 2010920618

Designed by RoS
Type set in Bremen Bd BT/Candara

ISBN: 978-0-7643-3457-3

Printed in China

DEDICATION

To my husband, Ralph,
the wind beneath my wings

Detail of The Friends in Mary's Garden by Jeannie Roulet Minchak

CONTENTS

FOREWORD

If you've ever planned to make a quilt, gotten partway through, and then abandoned the project, you need to read this book. It will give you hope. Pray that someone like author Mary Kerr discovers your incomplete relic, persuades her artist friends to revisit your work, and in the process elevates your partial quilt to heirloom status!

The premise of this book is charming and one all quilters can relate to: take old patchwork blocks, distribute them to artists with very few "rules" and see what these talented souls can do with the vintage textiles.

I wish I'd thought of it. Too often I've passed piles of patchwork blocks at an auction, hesitant to buy or change someone else's work. Now I know that socializing and creativity can start with the discovery of old quilt blocks and I'm tempted to start my own "Vintage Revisited" group. You can too since Mary gives easy to implement guidelines about how to gather like-minded souls and start "re-patching the world." The concept of Vintage Revisited is now within everyone's grasp.

Why is "Vintage Revisited" relevant today? For me it touches all the right heartstrings: re-making the old quilt blocks honors an anonymous artist of an earlier time but at the same time, it stretches the concept of what a quilt block is as individual modern artists re-form and complete the works. This is recycling and repurposing at its highest level. The months-long process of planning, altering the blocks, and creating new works unites the makers as they encourage each other. It challenges each quiltmaker to play and experiment–plus it's a great excuse for a party!

Mary Kerr has added something new to the craft of quiltmaking. In Vintage Revisited she gives us permission to work hand-in-hand with a long-gone quiltmaker and through a process of re-thinking the old piece, we are able to truly produce unique work today. Thank you, Mary.

Pepper Cory
Beaufort, North Carolina

PREFACE

For as long as women have been quilting, there have been projects left undone. Some quilts were never finished because of time constraints, others were not of the quality of workmanship desired, and still others were simply victims of a woman's prerogative to change her mind. As a result, we frequently find orphan blocks and block sets that have been saved over time. Few wanted to finish the projects, yet our thrifty nature would not allow them to be discarded.

I grew up in a family of quilters and was blessed to be the recipient of many, many unfinished projects. My two great-grandmothers, Crissie Agnes Say (1883-1969) and Frances Artis Cummins (1876–1969), quilted into their 90s and I remember thinking as a child that they were always busy. We had an abundance of quilts to keep us warm and I was shocked when I realized my childhood friends did not all have quilts on their beds. My own grandmothers, Kathryne Elizabeth Pickering Say (1911–2003) and Minnie Opal Cummins Wilson (1911–2007), followed the tradition of productivity. These women were raising families during the depression and war years. Like many from that era, they saved even the smallest scrap and never threw anything away.

The women in my family were prolific quilters who did not have time to finish everything they started. As the only grandchild who sews, I have been the fortunate recipient of many, if not all, of the unfinished projects from these four women. I received their unfinished blocks, partial tops, fabric scraps and extensive collections of sewing "stuff." Perhaps they thought that I could solve that construction puzzle, or find more of that particular shade of green, or find the time to finish the last few blocks in the set.

I have long enjoyed incorporating these leftover pieces into my contemporary work. I have finished some quilts as intended but more often I will combine blocks, attempt an innovative setting, or create a small quilt that showcases a limited number of blocks. I celebrate my

Detail of Baskets and Buttons by Mary Kerr

grandmothers and pay homage to the quilting traditions they passed on to me. I have collected vintage pieces for a number of years and have often collaborated with others on projects involving vintage textiles. Sometimes we simply exchanged ideas and other times we bought a set of blocks and divide them—leaving it up to the individual artist to design a final project.

Vintage Revisited was born in April 2006 when 22 quilters were invited to come and play. I wanted to see what would happen if a set of blocks were divided among a larger group of artists. This book is the story of these quilts and a celebration of the group of women who were invited to think outside of their normal design parameters. I share with you the quilts that these ladies created in this project, and I will address the unique challenges of working with vintage fabrics, groups, and timelines. I challenge others to start their own projects and exchanges. It truly is an adventure in which any quilter can participate.

I would like to thank the artists who worked with me, and I look forward to introducing you to these wonderful women in the following pages. Their selfless gift of time and talent went over and above the expectations of friendship. I was repeatedly humbled and amazed by their creations. I am thrilled to share their work in print.

Thank you to the staff at Schiffer Publishing, Ltd., for their co-operation and encouragement. Thank you to Barb Garrett and Sue Reich for their assistance during the photography phase. Thank you to Lori East, Cyndi Souder, and my sister, Karen Mitchell, for reading the manuscript and helping to organize my thoughts and syntax. Thank you to the members of the Quilters Professional Network who generously lent me their quilts for photography. And last, but not least, thank you to my family and to the women in my life who serve as my army of cheerleaders. Life would not be the same without you!

Mary Kerr

WHAT·IS·VINTAGE·REVISITED?

I DIDN'T THINK I CO ULD DO IT BUT I DID!!!

Detail of On Point by Pam Weeks

Throughout our history, a woman's work has never been completely done. As a result, many quilting projects have been left in various stages of completion. We find quilt tops, fragments, and an abundance of blocks. Lots of blocks! I call these unfinished projects orphans. They are the abandoned scraps that were never provided a finished place to call home.

I have a large collection of these orphans and I find myself drawn to the pieces that are damaged or poorly constructed. The price tags are palatable and I frequently incorporate the vintage textiles into my work. I have embarrassed my children for years by stopping at flea markets, thrift shops, junk shops and, yes, an occasional antique shop. The kids attended auctions while still in strollers and it was an astute four year old who once told a neighbor, "My Mommy buys lots of junk!"

As I played with these castoffs, I found myself trying different styles with identical blocks. I challenged myself to use blocks from the same orphan family in unique ways. I shared blocks with friends and loved seeing the design variations. I began to wonder what would happen if we divided a set of blocks among a larger group of artists? Would anyone else be interested?

In the spring of 2006, I sent out the following letter to 22 quilting friends with the expectation that only a limited number would be willing to play. My invitees were an eclectic mix of friends and quilting acquaintances.

Dear Friends and Fellow Quilters,

As many of you know, I have collaborated with others on a number of projects involving vintage textiles. We frequently buy a set of blocks and divide them –– leaving it up to the individual artist to design a final project.

I would like to expand this challenge concept to involve 12 or more quilters of all backgrounds. What would happen if we divide a set of blocks among us and let each of us go? The group I am envisioning includes art quilters, traditionalists, historians and relative newcomers to this quilting journey. I am sending this letter out to 22 of you and will work with whatever number of participants we have.

If you choose to participate, I plan to send out 6 sets of blocks over the next two years. Once you receive each block, you would have 4 months to complete a small wall hanging. The finished size is 24 x 24 and the only requirement is that the block be included in the finished product. You can add to it, cut it up, embellish it, recreate it, improve upon it –– whatever makes your heart sing!

I cannot promise anything but fun! At a minimum, I plan a traveling exhibit of selected pieces from the project –– as many as the individual quilt shows will allow. I would love to see our exhibit at several regional and/or national shows.

I will not be able to provide any monetary compensation, but your quilts will be yours to keep, sell or share after they are done traveling the world and (hopefully) being published. I will be responsible for purchasing the sets of blocks we will work with and will cover any expenses incurred with the traveling exhibit.

If you have the time, inclination, party spirit and willingness to participate, please let me know by May 1, 2006. I plan to send out the first set of blocks by May 15th. Comments, suggestions and concerns are welcome.

I look forward to working with as many of you as possible!

Mary

Much to my surprise, almost everyone wanted to play! Those who said no did so with deep regret and have continued to be vocal supporters of the project. I organized a group of 19 talented women who committed themselves to an exciting two-year project. We had no idea what we were getting ourselves into as Vintage Revisited was born.

Over the course of two years, I distributed six sets of vintage blocks to these adventurous artists. As I said in the original letter, the block was theirs to play with! They could add to it, cut it up, embellish it, recreate it, improve upon it, and more. The only requirements were that the finished quilt be their original design, that it measure 24 x 24 inches, and that the original block be included in the final project. I also made a 20th quilt using the leftover blocks from the project. These extra quilts are a variety of sizes. In all, there are 117 quilts.

I am honored to share this journey in print. And now, the quilts.

Mary hanging A Pennsylvania Sampler by Barbara Garrett.
Photo courtesy of Cyndi Souder

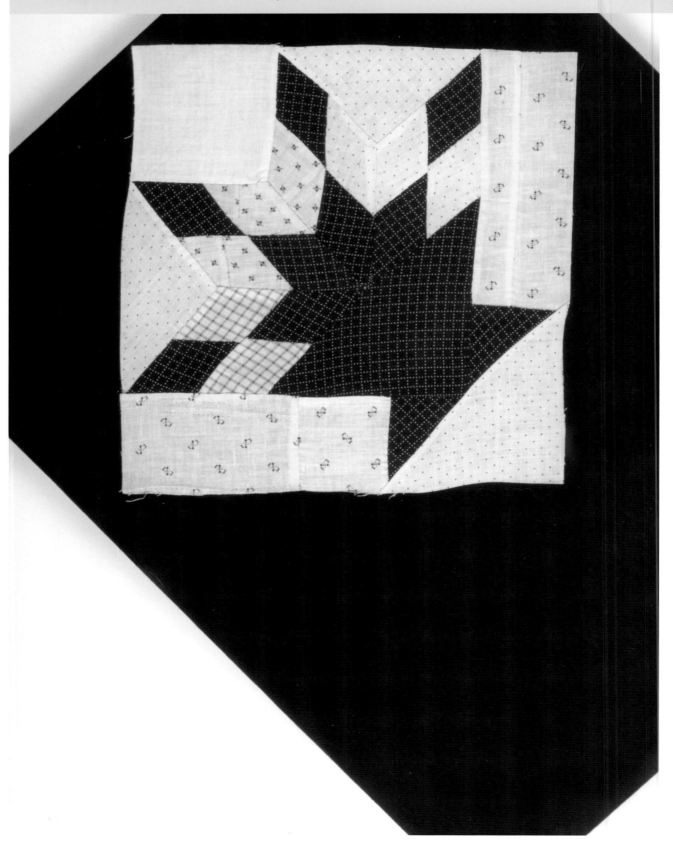

The first orphan block the participants received was an indigo and white basket block that was typical of blocks created in early 1900. They came from a set of 30 blocks - all dark blues with white shirting fabrics. The basket pattern was consistent, but each block used a different combination of fabrics. Some were better constructed than others!

My letter to the artists read:

"Now that you have received your block — it is yours to play with! You can add to it, cut it up, embellish it, recreate it, improve upon it, and more. The only requirements are that the block be included in the finished project and that you have fun. The quilt needs to measure 24 x 24."

The quilters received this first block in May of 2006 and were given four months to complete their small quilt. Many were concerned with the "rules" (or lack thereof) and most chose to be very conservative with this first project. Some were not comfortable deconstructing their block and others were unable to wrap their brains around altering another woman's work.

Jane Miller said, "I hadn't been able to take apart the block. Something about 'destroying' someone else's hard work was unsettling, and my 'tribute' to an unknown quilter would be that this small piece of her (or his!) life would remain intact for perpetuity."

Pam Weeks said, "[When] the first block came, and I put it up on my design wall, and every time I walked past, it would talk to me. 'Cut me! Cut me!' the basket called. I never believed in using vintage textiles beyond using them to teach about fabrics and styles, but this exercise really changed my outlook."

Several participants wanted more structure and chose to create their own set of personal rules. Both Barb Garrett and Kathy Metelica decided to use only vintage fabrics in their quilts. Judy Gula chose to feature vintage linens in her quilts and Karen Dever incorporated her signature piping into each of her designs.

As the quilts began to arrive at my home in August and September, I realized we had an amazing project on our hands. They were beautifully constructed, thoughtfully planned, and a joy to examine. I expected a variety of designs. but this collection was exciting!

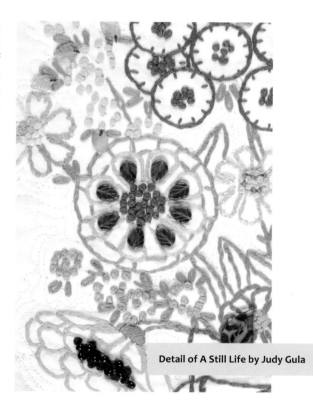

Detail of A Still Life by Judy Gula

Detail of Riches by Paula Golden

Doris Bloomer
What Once Was Old is New Again
hand and machine pieced, hand quilted

    Receiving the first block of the challenge in the mail was very exciting. Having never made a quilt without a pattern proved to be quite a challenge but I was pleased with the result and the quilt actually turned out to be square! In order to finish it on time I took the quilt with me to Germany when I went to visit my family. What a thrill to share this project with them and hear their thoughts and ideas as well.

◆　◆　◆　◆　◆

Linda Cooper
Mary's Floral Tribute
hand and machine pieced, machine appliquéd, hand and machine quilted

    It was very satisfying to use such a beautiful basket block. I added a painted background (done Phil Beaver style) and then filled it with a great bouquet of broderie-perse flowers. I cut the flowers from a decorator print and machine-appliquéd them with variegated thread. I dissected light sections of the basket block and painted in the different colors. I dedicate this quilt to Mary Kerr for the brilliant idea of using these old blocks and challenging a group of quilters with a variety of styles to do their best.

Karen Dever

A Tisket and Tasket, A Blue and White Basket
hand and machine pieced, machine quilted

I have always enjoyed working with fabric and different block designs to create that one-of-a-kind textile. This quilt was my first attempt at working with a vintage textile and I was leery of doing anything unique. Using the repro fabrics that I love, I kept the basket intact and accented with piping.

◆ ◆ ◆ ◆ ◆

Bonnie Dwyer

Patriotic Basket
hand and machine pieced, hand quilted

This first block spoke to me immediately as the center of a traditional "red, white, and blue" quilt. It represents my usual working style: traditional piecing, employing a rather standard setting, and hand quilting. I used vintage fabrics and some small vintage basket blocks I had in my collection. I then quilted it by hand to unite the elements into a very traditional quilt.

Lori East
Goodness Gracious
hand and machine pieced, machine quilted

Before this challenge I was an "incomplete" quilter. I rarely finished anything, and never showed a single quilt. Either my inner critic or plain old boredom got me. But time was short and I could not overthink this challenge. I just ran with nothing more than a mental image of the finished quilt, cutting and sewing intuitively and almost carelessly. The energy in "spiky things," has always seemed joyous and so this piece became a sort of portal for me. It opened a door to the goofy, sappy joy that comes from doing things just for the fun of it.

◆　◆　◆　◆　◆

Lisa Ellis
Quilt Block Scramble
hand and machine pieced, machine quilted

This quilt is a puzzle. Can you solve it? It's harder than it looks. (Hint: Use the setting squares in the sashing, as a clue for how to place each piece.) The pieces are attached to the felt background using Velcro circles. I made the pieces by first creating the top and fusing it to a thick interfacing. Then I fused a piece of fabric to the back of the interfacing and chopped it up in equal-size squares.

Barbara Garrett
Indigo Basket
hand pieced, hand quilted

As a quilt historian, I had difficulty with the thought of undoing another woman's work so I needed to find a way to keep the original block intact and build from there. Setting the basket on point and surrounding it with several borders seemed to me a logical alternative. I decided that for the six quilts of this project, I would use only fabric that is age-appropriate to each original block. The vintage indigo, double pink, brown and shirting fabrics complimented the basket nicely and created a quilt with a circa 1900 feel.

◆　◆　◆　◆　◆

Paula Golden
Riches
hand and machine pieced, machine appliquéd, machine quilted

The starting point for this quilt was the blue and white basket block, circa 1900. I used vintage rickrack and a hand-embroidered doily in the design that reflects the beauty and bounty of a summer garden.

Judy Gula
A Still Life – Flowers in Oriental Vase
hand and machine pieced, hand embellished, machine quilted

When I received this first block, I honestly did not even "see" the basket pattern, only the fabric colors. Blue and white make me think of Japanese indigo-dyed fabrics. I used several Japanese fabrics I have been collecting in the scrappy border and then found the beautiful vintage embroidery which had an Oriental look to it. I used free-motion stitching to make the embroidery motif pop, and beading to embellish the flowers. Thus began my challenge-within-a-challenge, to use vintage embroidery with Mary's vintage blocks.

◆　◆　◆　◆　◆

Mary Kerr
A Basket for Cyndi Lou
hand and machine pieced, machine quilted

The excitement of this two-year project was mixed with a healthy dose of apprehension as I worked on this first quilt. I was thrilled to have 19 talented women who were willing to come and "play" with me, but was nervous about the overall coordination of people, quilts, and events. This first quilt is totally unlike anything I have ever done. The block was cut into strips and woven with the remnants of a friend's childhood skirt. It was set in medallion setting with scraps of a postage stamp quilt from 1890.

Kathy Lincoln
A Basket Full of Geese
hand and machine pieced, machine quilted

    I was not prepared to cut apart or change the basket block. I went to my stash to find appropriate reproduction fabrics to match and, of course, that did involve some additional acquisition. I love pieced borders so I added my favorite flying geese border, and set the block on point.

◆ ◆ ◆ ◆ ◆

Kathy Metelica
Indigo Center Star
hand and machine pieced, machine quilted

    I have been "blending the old with the new" since my introduction to Paul Pilgrim. Each time that a challenge block is given to me, I try to incorporate other vintage blocks and fabrics from that time period into the quilt. I am a true believer that quilt blocks were made to be put into a quilt. For those blocks that never "grew up," my task is to find them a home. This indigo basket became an Indigo star when I paired it with period fabrics from my collection.

Jane Miller
Old Blue
hand and machine pieced, machine quilted

    This first Vintage Revisited project had me feeling both honored to have been chosen, yet apprehensive about my ability to meet the challenge. Mary had promised to eventually return this finished project, so a name for the quilt emerged as it was completed. I'm gratified to have this small block from the past completed, and felt an appropriate title would be "Something Borrowed, Something Blue; Something Old and Something New", or simply "Old Blue".

◆   ◆   ◆   ◆   ◆

Jeannie Roulet Minchak
Homage to Florence
hand and machine pieced, hand appliquéd, hand quilted, 35x36 inches

    When I saw Florence Peto's vintage scrap quilt in the Shelburne Museum, I was so taken with it that I knew someday I would try and adapt her idea. When someone gave me a box of very old scraps, I knew I would use them for this project. I was inspired by Florence's belief that old scraps aren't to be stuck away in boxes but used to create new and beautiful quilts. I'm not a big fan of broderie perse or trapunto, so I adapted her appliqué designs by using three-dimensional fabric flowers and leaves. This quilt combines the very old scraps with reproduction fabrics, all surrounding the vintage basket block in the center!

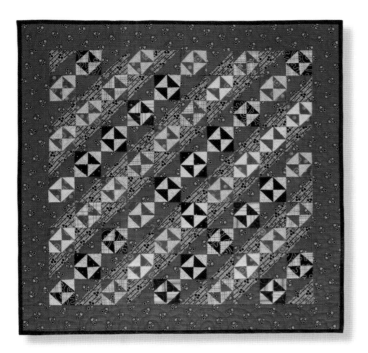

Jeannette Muir
June Lucille
machine pieced, machine quilted

The pieced basket in this first challenge was perfect for my style. I was delighted because I am a piecer, through and through. One of my favorite pastimes, and therapy, is picking apart old blocks and tops, especially someone else's, not mine. Apart it came! In my "stash" there are countless small fabric scraps from the turn of the century (the last one), and lots of the red print salvaged from a previous "organ donor". This quilt was completed almost immediately and I love it!

◆　◆　◆　◆　◆

Sue Reich
Morris in the Garden
hand and machine pieced, hand embroidered, hand quilted, hand appliquéd

My inspiration in the development of this quilt was the William Morris style fabric that I used as the background fabric. It was purchased at a store in London. I tried to use every bit of the original block by appliquéing the basket and creating the petals from the remaining white pieces. The quilt is embellished with antique laces and a late nineteenth-century spider web block from my collection.

Shannon Shirley
Amber Leaves
hand and machine pieced, machine quilted

When I committed to make six quilts for Mary's Vintage Revisited challenge, I had no idea what was in store! I paired the leaf batik with the vintage basket in this traditional setting.

◆ ◆ ◆ ◆ ◆

Cyndi Souder
A Tisket, A Tasket, A Little Vintage Basket
hand and machine pieced, hand inked, machine quilted

I don't do vintage. I couldn't imagine a tougher challenge than to take this block that is so obviously old and make the finished work look like the art quilts that I generally make. I struggled for ideas and then decided to stop fighting the block. It wanted to be a basket, and so I added the batiks that I love so much and let the basket be a basket. I guess now I have to say I DO do vintage.

Pam Weeks
On Point
hand and machine pieced, hand and machine quilted

I had a long-held belief that vintage fabric and blocks should remain as found–unfinished and preserved for the next generation. This challenge has changed my mind. The basket block hung on my design wall begged me to let go and cut it in half. I did, and to my delight, I was freed to play with antique fabric. I found blocks in my stash to complement the fabric and style of the basket and worked the words in my head until the right sound and rhythm matched the design.

◆　◆　◆　◆　◆

Mary Kerr
Baskets and Buttons
hand and machine pieced, machine appliquéd, machine quilted by Shannon Shirley, 28x28 inches

I took the remaining eight basket blocks and made them into this sweet wall hanging. Four blocks were left intact and the remaining blocks were dissected and used to form the multiple borders. Buttons from my grandmothers were used as embellishment. They were my first quilt teachers and my constant source of inspiration.

The second round of the project called for the artists to work with poorly constructed Odd Fellow blocks that are circa 1880. They were from a set of 30 blocks I purchased on eBay. This was one of those instances where the seller definitely took pictures of the best blocks and chose to leave out some important details, but I loved them anyway.

These blocks were received with mixed reviews. I personally loved the cheddar and teal colors, but not everyone shared my sentiments. Barb Garrett and I believe that orange is a neutral color and can go with anything. Others saw the orange and green as drab solids that had seen better days. One of my artists even called to tell me it looked like, "…a dog's breakfast"!

While working on this set of quilts, many of our artists had their own personal "ah-ha" moments. Kathy Lincoln said:

"One of the things that I enjoyed most was that I had to think out of my very comfortable box. I had to explore and learn and then put into action." And Linda Cooper said, *"Mary's Quilt Challenge provided me with an opportunity to push past the limits of my previous quilts."*

Some artists took the opportunity to try new techniques and others worked with colors they had never considered. Still others created quilts that were very personal and moving. Most found new confidence as we were able to view images of each others work on my website. We were all in awe as we appreciated the variety of talent, design, and creativity.

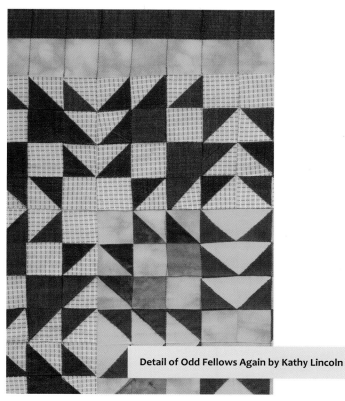

Detail of Odd Fellows Again by Kathy Lincoln

Detail of Mediterranean Sea by Shannon Shirley

The Second Set of Quilts

Doris Bloomer
Patience – Outside the Box
machine pieced, hand appliquéd, hand quilted

   Getting the blocks in the mail is almost like opening presents on Christmas morning. When I received the second block I knew I wanted it to be a sampler quilt. Drafting my plan and picking complementary blocks on a piece of paper turned out to be very easy. Then came the picking of the fabric – an almost impossible task! The colors were so bold - not something I usually work with. I became so frustrated I completely stopped working on it. And then, something clicked and the colors came together like a dream. Success!! Thank you to Lori Smith for her wonderful appliqué patterns.

◆   ◆   ◆   ◆   ◆

Linda Cooper
The Joker's Always Wild
machine pieced, machine appliquéd, hand painted, machine quilted

   Mary's quilt challenge has provided me with an opportunity to push past the limits of my previous quilts. I've played with partial faces in my work before and this time decided to just do it. I painted my background (Phil Beaver-style), and appliquéd my joker with the flying geese of the Odd Fellow's block recut and paper-pieced in the jester's hat. He has a 3-D, gathered collar, and is waving hello to all with a tracing of my hand. The Joker is also a tribute quilt to all the fine card-playing family members and friends that I've known.

Karen Dever
Not Odd Anymore
machine pieced, machine quilted

After viewing what other participants did with their blocks in the first round, I became braver and I took this block apart, cleaned up the pieces and paper pieced the Odd Fellows block, adding in contemporary batiks to repeat the block. Can you find the original?

◆　◆　◆　◆　◆

Bonnie Dwyer
In The English Tradition
machine pieced, hand and machine quilted

In my quilting journey, I have studied a number of early English patchwork quilts. The center medallion is a style that is frequently used to utilize scraps and spare blocks. The flying geese block for round #2 seemed perfect for this style. I incorporated the geese blocks into the borders, along with other scraps from my stash. I now have a better understanding of, and appreciation for, this style quilt.

Lori East
Red and Green Make Orange
machine pieced, machine quilted

I found the colors of the original block exciting visually, but I fought with them. These are not the colors I would choose from the big box of Crayons! But they **can** play well together. And, even though I struggle with structure, I do need boundaries to keep me in line. When I think I have a "better" idea, the thing I'm working on has a tendency to run amok, and not in a good way. Using black and white with the other colors built in contrast and structure and gave discipline to both my imagination and the finished piece.

◆　◆　◆　◆　◆

Lisa Ellis
Are You in or Out?
machine pieced, machine appliquéd, hand embellished, machine quilted

For me, as an art quilter, working with traditional quilt concepts is way outside my comfort box. I sort of skipped the traditional quilting phase. For this quilt challenge, I decided to learn some new techniques, like setting a block on point and calculating the setting triangles. I relearned how to make a Seminole border. Wow – going around corners is tough! I used more traditional machine quilting too. But then at the end, I incorporated my usual stuff: raw edge appliqué triangles, free motion thread play and some hot fix crystals (phew – that felt much better).

Barbara Garrett
A Pennsylvania Sampler
machine pieced, hand quilted

The bright crayon colors of late 19th century Pennsylvania German quilts form my favorite color palette. I love variety in my piecing, so decided a traditional sampler style of some favorite blocks would be the best way for me to keep the integrity of the original block, in a slightly smaller size. By using vintage fabric, I was able to make a quilt reminiscent of those made in the 1890s in my area of southeastern Pennsylvania. Since combining fabrics and colors are my favorite parts of the quiltmaking process, creating many different blocks multiplied my fun.

◆　◆　◆　◆　◆

Paula Golden
A Statement For Peace
machine pieced, hand appliquéd, machine quilted

If we could learn to treat each other with kindness and tolerance, I believe world peace would soon follow. The game board design represents the hope we can learn to play together. The quilting designs support the theme: the continents of earth are stitched on the turquoise circles as the sun shines; birds of peace circle the game board and the Ethics of Reciprocity (AKA the Golden Rule) is quilted in the borders.

Judy Gula
A Basket of Water Lilies
machine pieced, hand embellished, machine quilted

My second quilt in the challenge features a vintage embroidery piece that is embellished with angelina fibers, sheers, and beads. A Log Cabin pieced border bubbles in the water and is contained by the vintage block fragments at the corners.

◆　◆　◆　◆　◆

Mary Kerr
Orange is a Neutral Color
hand and machine pieced, machine quilted

I was excited about this second set of quilt blocks as I love the bold colors of the fabrics from 1880. Orange is one of my favorite colors and I have an extensive collection of vintage orange pieces. My challenge quilt includes another period quilt block and fragments of a tattered quilt top from the 1940s. The orange prairie points and the solid red fabrics are contemporary additions. This quilt is positive proof that orange is definitely a neutral color!

Kathy Lincoln
Odd Fellows Again
machine pieced, machine quilted

The original block was one of the Odd Fellows variations and so I decided to look at the other variations for inspiration. Once I found the one that I liked the best, I had to determine how to adapt the original block to the new block. The only way it would work was to reverse the light and dark fabrics. Once the center block was finished, I designed the borders to echo the Odd Fellows block in waves from the mid points on each side.

◆　◆　◆　◆　◆

Kathy Metelica
Vintage Cheddar Sampler
hand and machine pieced, machine quilted

I am very excited to have had this opportunity to join Mary Kerr and her quilt block challenge. In this second round, I paired this Odd Fellows blocks with three other cheddar blocks from the 1880s. They are set with period fabrics from my collection.

Jane Miller
Playing Hide and Seek With the Geese at the Zoo
machine pieced, machine quilted

As one of the least experienced quilters in this group, I'm continually stretched to meet each challenge. Oh, what to do with the "Cheddar Cheese" block? Several friends suggested batik fabrics, but after purchasing several various pieces, nothing "spoke" to me. At a quilt shop in Madison, Virginia, these zoo animals caught my eye with their perfect combination of deep teals and oranges. Among the "flying geese" of the block, I pictured the animals playing hide and seek throughout the jungle scene. Then, I just had to fashion separate animals for small fingers to tuck into the triangular pockets around block.

◆　◆　◆　◆　◆

Jeannie Roulet Minchak
Two Friends
machine pieced, hand appliquéd, machine quilted

The contemporary colors of this antique block had me racing to my stash...to pull out a hand-dyed batik I was saving for just the right moment. The borders were created using paper-piecing and appliqué. I love how the old and new blend together so beautifully...like two friends. This quilt honors my artist friend Nancy Marstaller...we create beautiful music whenever we're together.

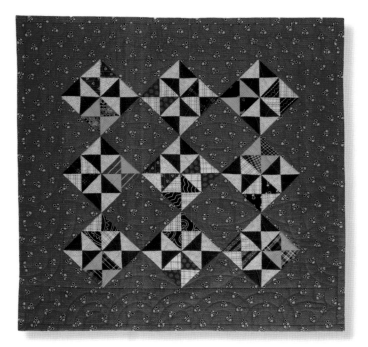

Jeannette Muir
Arabelle
machine pieced, machine quilted

When the Odd Fellows block arrived, I couldn't resist picking it apart. I even forgot to take a photograph. Picking apart old tops has long been a favorite, relaxing process for me. This block was so small that I had the luxury of adding a multitude of vintage fabrics. The tiny cheddar half-squares were stitched together to make larger units. Fabrics left over from other "pickers" made up the pinwheel units. The wonderful vintage red print, also used in other challenge projects, provided the main background and border.

◆   ◆   ◆   ◆   ◆

Sue Reich
High in the Sky
hand and machine pieced, hand appliquéd, hand quilted

I never loved the color orange until my youngest daughter became a Princeton Tiger field hockey player. For four years, my wardrobe acquired more and more orange. Now, I use orange/cheddar in my quilts and you will always find orange sparkles in my garden. When I received the Flying Geese square, I knew immediately what I intended to make. The geese would be flying south in formation as they always do in the fall over my Connecticut home. I dug deep into my fabric stash to complement the orange with purple and burgundy prints.

Shannon Shirley
Mediterranean Sea
machine pieced, machine appliquéd, machine embroidered, machine quilted

In October 2006, I went on a Mediterranean cruise. We had six ports of call in Spain, France, and Italy. While on a daytrip in Livorno, Italy, I saw a cheddar-colored house and knew instantly it would be the subject of my challenge quilt. I colored a picture while still on board to capture the inspiration, and immediately started the project when I got home. The pieces were fused in place, starting at the top. I then free-motion embroidered all the details and, finally, free-motion quilted it.

◆　◆　◆　◆　◆

Cyndi Souder
It's About Time
machine pieced, machine appliquéd, hand embellished, machine quilted

The subject of time often creeps into my work. In this case, I was behind schedule completing this quilt and I still hadn't come up with a design! Fresh from a Melody Johnson class at Quilt Surface Design Symposium, I decided to approach the project with fusible and whimsy. Working quickly, I created three wheels and then got out my hardware embellishments: keys, clock parts, and other assorted treasures. I made design decisions as I came to each step, working without a sketch or vision of the finished piece. I love the quilt and I actually enjoyed working without a net.

Pam Weeks
Two Roads Diverged
machine pieced, machine quilted

When the block for a challenge comes, it goes up on my wall and stays there until it begins to speak to me. This one started talking right away about roads not taken and the flying geese units became paths leading away. Suddenly the lines from the Robert Frost poem, The Road Not Taken came into my head and the design for the roads diverging in a yellow wood just clicked.

◆ ◆ ◆ ◆ ◆

Mary Kerr
All Worn Out
hand and machine pieced, machine quilted by Marie Tallman, 48x69 inches

This quilt was designed when I took the remaining nine Odd Fellows blocks and paired them with contemporary orange fabrics and remnants of a 1940s quilt top. The green border was a well-loved linen skirt from my closet. All the components had former lives and I was thrilled to bring them back from being All Worn Out!

*T*he third set of quilts was due to be completed in the summer, so the Americana themed blocks seemed very appropriate. The blocks are the Double Fan pattern, and are constructed from a variety of red, white, and blue fabrics, circa 1900. I purchased this set of 39 blocks when The Mid-Atlantic Quilt Festival show was still held in Williamsburg, Virginia.

There were minimal complaints about these blocks in spite of the fact that many were stained and most were not square. Most of the group had embraced the idea of dissecting the blocks and the creative juices were flowing freely.

Cyndi Souder said, "In the beginning, I tried to respect the original pattern and keep it recognizable. Once I saw what everyone else was doing, I realized that I could do whatever I wanted. By the third block, I'd reach for the seam ripper as I opened the package. Using vintage fabrics became sort of a game. What would I have to do to the fabric so that I could I hide it in a quilt that I enjoyed making?"

Lisa Ellis's quilt," Balls in the Air," received national acclaim when it was juried into the International Quilt Association's special exhibit in Houston that featuring patriotic quilts. Her special quilt was featured on the IQA website and was our only quilt brave enough to travel solo.

This set was probably the most diverse set of quilts in the project, and has been especially well received at the various venues and shows. Everyone seems to respond to red, white, and blue.

Detail of Carmen by Bonnie Dwyer

Detail of Thinking of Betsy by Doris Bloomer

Detail of Balls in the Air by Lisa Ellis

Doris Bloomer
Thinking of Betsy
hand pieced, machine pieced, hand appliquéd, hand quilted

The challenge for me has been to try to experiment a little more with each block. This time I decided to go a little farther and take the block apart so I could use the pieces individually. When I received the block it was the middle of the summer here in Georgia, and close to the July 4th holiday. The inspiration for *Thinking of Betsy* came from the red, white, and blue color scheme of the block and all the patriotic decorations you can see everywhere in this area during that time of the year. Naming the quilt *Betsy Ross* just fit!

◆ ◆ ◆ ◆ ◆

Linda Cooper
A Quilter's Caravan
machine pieced, hand and machine appliquéd, machine quilted

A bundle of Kimiko's Chinoiserie fabrics helped me turn the red, white, and blue block into this carriage. I had a good time appliquéing elements from the collection by hand and machine to decorate the cart. It was also fun to add the beads. The background is an ombre fabric from McKenna Ryan. I left out much of the undercarriage and my engineer sons would tell me that I made it non-functional. That's why it's named, *A Quilter's Caravan*– it can travel only straight from one quilt shop to another.

Karen Dever
Fan Flower
machine pieced, hand appliquéd, machine quilted

Now I am not afraid of anything!! I washed the original block, took it apart and reused pieces of the fabric to create my "Fan Flower!" For an added touch, I used part of a doily that my grandmother made for embellishment.

◆   ◆   ◆   ◆   ◆

Bonnie Dwyer
Carmen
machine pieced, machine appliquéd, machine quilted

Having seen some "outside the box" quilts of others in this challenge, I felt it was time to do something less traditional with block number three. I think I succeeded. While looking at this block on my design wall for several weeks, the "hat" concept kept returning, and with it a mental image of Brazilian singer and actress Carmen Miranda. I did a little research and found the famous Latin singer always had fruits in her wild hats, which she made herself. Fussy-cut novelty fruit and flower fabrics adorn the hat in this quilt to achieve a much wilder result than is my norm.

Lori East
Real Life
Hand and machine pieced, machine quilted

This quilt is exactly like real life to me: I seem to always be dealing with bits and pieces of things that seem to not go together easily. So I "cut and paste," and fix and patch, and sometimes try to make things look better than they are. I try to wait and see how things will turn out (although waiting isn't my strength). Mostly though, I just have faith that in the end things will work out and I'll end up with something wonderful. It might be messy and it might be unexpected, but it will always be interesting.

◆　◆　◆　◆　◆

Lisa Ellis
Keeping the Balls in the Air
machine pieced, hand and machine appliquéd, machine quilted

With elections around the corner, and issues hotly debated, we are keenly aware of the challenges in managing our country's affairs. In this quilt, Uncle Sam is trying to keep all the balls in the air. The Crime and Health circles are cut from fans from the antique block. My husband, Mike, drew the image of Uncle Sam that I used to design the appliqué.

Barbara Garrett
Night Flight
machine pieced, hand quilted

Pink, indigo, and shirting fabrics form a popular color palette from the late 19th century. The original two fans were dismantled, and four similar fans stitched from their pieces. These were supplemented with additional vintage fabric to form the four cornerstones of the quilt. Thus elements of the original block pattern were included in the quilt. The floating stars arrangement in the center of the quilt was inspired by a mid-19th century crib quilt I once admired in an exhibit. I liked the flying geese pattern as a base for the border design and to complement the center of the quilt.

◆　　◆　　◆　　◆　　◆

Paula Golden
A River Runs Through
hand and machine pieced, machine quilted

What are the themes that connect generations? In the reworking of an antique, skewed, feathered star block, the remnants of seven quilters' fabrics and blocks were combined to create this quilt. The central blue area of the fan block represents the love of quilting that connects many lives.

Judy Gula
The Little Dutch Girl
hand and machine pieced, hand embellished, machine quilted

The Little Dutch Girl contains the original vintage block and additional vintage fabrics in the scrappy border. The vintage linen is different this time because it does not include embroidery. A vintage hand towel and found objects complete the picture. The hunt for all things Dutch was part of the fun: included is a vintage Dutch trim, blue and white porcelain shoes, buttons with windmills, and tulip beads.

Mary Kerr
Cheers for the Red White and Blue
hand and machine pieced, machine appliquéd, machine quilted by Shannon Shirley

This quilt was inspired by the unique fly foot design in my block's red fabric. This design has fallen out of favor since the atrocities of the Nazi regime, but it has been a popular motif throughout time. I chose not to pass out any blocks to the group participants that contained this particular fabric, and had not planned to use them in the exhibit. When I found the star block in my collection, however, with the same red fabric, the design wheels started turning. The top is constructed with parts of six different quilts from the early 1900s. The binding is vintage fabrics from 1880 and the backing is a fragment of a damaged top from the 1940s.

Kathy Lincoln
Flags of Our Mothers
hand and machine pieced, machine quilted

The double fan block was a wonderful inspiration. I had a lot of fun with this block. I had a new curved piecing template so I decided to play. Instead of piecing the fan I pieced the background. I tried to keep to reproduction fabrics so that the flavor of the quilt would remain the same. The border was just trimmed blocks.

◆　◆　◆　◆　◆

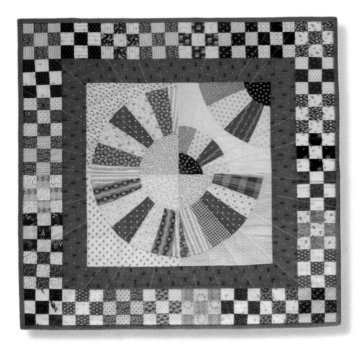

Kathy Metelica
Fractured Fans
hand and machine pieced, machine quilted

I incorporated other vintage fan blocks from my collection to complete this piece. It's wonderful to bring orphaned blocks together and find them a home in a quilt. It's as if the blocks grew up and became a family.

Jane Miller
Beach Balls
hand and machine pieced, machine appliquéd, machine quilted

    With enthusiasm I opened the envelope containing our third challenge. When I saw the red, white, and blue semicircles, my first thought was "Beach Balls." Still believing it important to maintain the block as a whole unit, I carefully reassembled the curved edges and frayed pieces. It was fun searching for, and finding, fabrics that would recreate another beach ball, and I was delighted to find the sand pails for the outer border. The starfish was added for whimsy.

◆ ◆ ◆ ◆ ◆

Jeannie Roulet Minchak
They Came to America
machine pieced, machine quilted

    When I first saw the original block, the words, "patriotic," and "United States of America," came to mind. When I found the border fabric, it reminded me of, "Old World," and what looked like flags in the windows. As an amateur genealogist, I have been moved and humbled by the stories of my husband's and my family's trek to the United States. This quilt honors these ancestors, and all those who left their homeland to follow the often winding path to the United States in search of opportunity and a brighter future.

Jeannette Muir
Rumiko
machine pieced, machine quilted

    This challenge was not as easy as the first two projects: I had to think! Before that, however, I took it apart. What made it a bit more difficult was the fact that the two curved motifs were unequal in size.
    Because this Drunkard's Path variation block was so tiny, it needed larger pieces of fabric. Nothing in my same-vintage stash was suitable, so I finally decided to cut up some of my precious yukatas. I must have saved them specifically for this purpose!

◆   ◆   ◆   ◆   ◆

Sue Reich
A More Fanciful Time
hand and machine pieced, hand appliquéd, hand embellished, hand quilted

    I designed this red, white, and blue quilt using EQ6. The silhouette appliqué also came from EQ6. The neckline is trimmed with antique lace from my collection of vintage textiles. Once again, I tried to use the entire original block provided for the challenge. The ruched flower was a white background I had cut away from the fans. I particularly like the fabric with the women's faces.

Shannon Shirley
Red, White, and Blue Sue
hand and machine pieced, hand and machine appliquéd, hand embellished, machine quilted

*I love my second quilt, Mediterranean Sea.
However, I felt the character of the block was lost,
so I knew I wanted to take that into consideration
when designing this quilt. Sue's bonnet, hand,
apron and shoes are the original block. I used a
variety of appliqué and quilting methods.*

◆ ◆ ◆ ◆ ◆

Cyndi Souder
We'll Always Have Paris
machine pieced, machine appliquéd, hand
stamped, hand inked, machine quilted

*Once again, I was absolutely stumped by
the block. The fabrics (after I deconstructed the
block) reminded me of the stripe that edges an
old airmail envelope. From there, I imagined a correspondence with a mysterious stranger in Paris. I
hand-stamped the organza in the background and
printed the vintage French airmail stamp directly
onto fabric. I used black and brown pens to hand
stipple the cancellation to match a stamp I used
in the background. The envelope is addressed to
my father, Cecil C. Zacheis, Port Penn, Del. Look for
his address stamp in the background.*

Pam Weeks
ET Phone Home
hand and machine pieced, machine quilted

    This goofy little block had a major sense of humor and, for whatever reason, the words began dancing in my head the moment I pulled more blocks from my stash and started to play. The letter blocks jumped up beside each other on the wall forming "ET" and then the house block came to the top of a pile of vintage fabric as "home." The circles in the challenge block became the umbrella contraption that ET constructed to phone his mother ship for a ride home.

◆   ◆   ◆   ◆   ◆

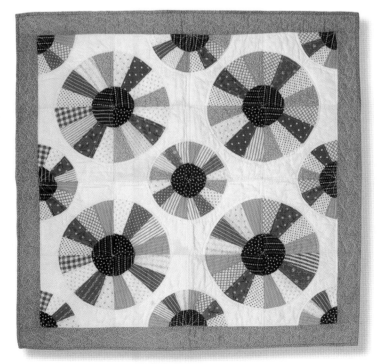

Mary Kerr
Circle the Wagons
hand and machine pieced, machine quilted by Linda Hahn, 33x33 inches

    I put the remaining 16 double fan blocks into this unique setting without sashing. It reminds me of wagon wheels. Can you imagine what the whole quilt would have looked like? Most of these blocks were in very poor condition so the entire quilt was tea-dyed after quilting to hide the significant stains.

The blocks for the fourth set of quilts were from a set of 36 blocks I purchased several years ago on eBay. Circa 1940, they are all the same pattern in solid yellow and white fabrics. This pattern has been called multiple names through the years, including Monkey Wrench, Churn Dash, Shoofly, and Hole in the Barn Door. In her book, *Encyclopedia of Quilt Patterns*, Barbara Brackman lists over 20 different titles for this design.

I expected that the color combination would appeal to most of my artists, but to my surprise, most were less than enamored with these blocks. They were poorly constructed and the fabric was very thin. The blocks ranged in size from eight to ten inches, so it is no surprise that this project was never completed by the original maker. I struggled to make the worst of the blocks fit into the 20th quilt, "A Crooked Barn."

Regardless, the creative juices continued to flow. Lori East said:

"It was with block #4 that I began to really GET IT that the quilt police weren't coming to my door to get me for using some atypical material in my quilt. I had cut up the block almost beyond recognition, just to figuratively grin at that voice that kept saying, 'It won't work.' The quilt is so not beautiful but it represents a different kind of success for me."

Paula Golden chose to work with fragments of a woman's sewing basket for her quilt. She said, "It has been an honor to be able to continue the legacy of quiltmaking in America by being part of Mary's Vintage Revisited. How often is one able to incorporate bra extenders, quilt blocks, dress pieces, and petroglyphs in one design?" Over the span of the Vintage Revisited project, Paula was completing her Masters of Interdisciplinary Studies program at Virginia Commonwealth University. Several of the pieces from her thesis exhibit echoed the images we enjoy in this quilt.

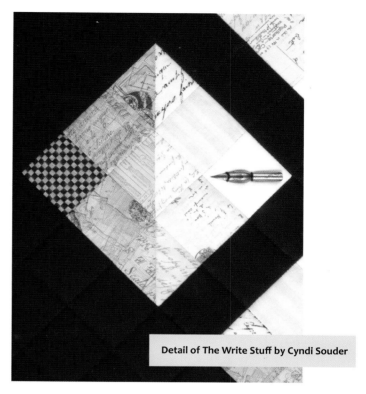

Detail of The Write Stuff by Cyndi Souder

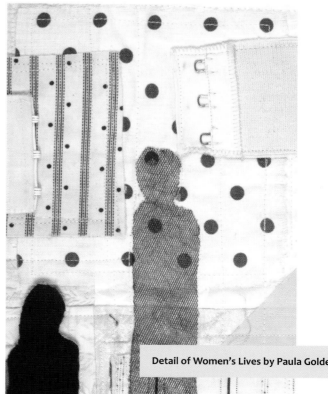

Detail of Women's Lives by Paula Golden

The Fourth Set of Quilts

Doris Bloomer
At the Lake
machine pieced, machine appliquéd, hand quilted

Every year a group of friends and I get together and travel to the Mid-Atlantic Quilt Fest in Hampton, Virginia. There are always so many new ideas and gadgets it boggles the mind. Last year I found this nifty little template that is designed to make scrap quilts easier. "Easy" is my style.... and I always wanted to make a true scrap quilt, therefore this was just perfect. I picked blue fabric for our lake and added the flower to incorporate Mary's block into the quilt. After all, there is always something blooming in Georgia, even during the winter.

◆　◆　◆　◆　◆

Linda Cooper
Zinnias by Yim
machine pieced, machine appliquéd, hand inked, hand embellished, machine quilted

My friends Diane and Cal Yim grow beautiful flowers, and Diane took a picture of their glorious zinnias. I've wanted to try to make it into a quilt and the great yellow and white from the challenge block was the incentive to finally make it. I added my hand-dyed fabrics and, with Tsukineko inks, painted the appliqués to look like the enlarged picture. I broderie-perse appliquéd the flowers with variegated thread and used an overlay method taught by Sherri Alcorn for placement. It was hard to know when to stop beading.

Karen Dever
Vintage Tulip
machine pieced, machine appliquéd, machine quilted

The original block was a solid yellow and white Churn Dash; this one was a challenge! Again I took the block apart and made half-square triangle units. I used a circa-1940 machine appliquéd tulip block as my focus and added repro fabrics with the original yellow and white to create, "Vintage Tulip."

◆　◆　◆　◆　◆

Bonnie Dwyer
Amethyst Vase
machine pieced, machine appliquéd, machine quilted

This quilt represents an early effort for me in the art quilt genre. I began the center medallion block in a workshop with quilt artist Marilyn Belford in the summer of 2007 at the New England Images show. Since the yellow elements in this block worked well with the yellow churn dash challenge block, I decided to work the challenge block into a series of borders. I incorporated coordinating yellows and purples into concentric borders to create an impression of a framed and matted image.

Lori East
Wallflowers
machine pieced, hand and machine appliquéd,
hand embellished, machine quilted

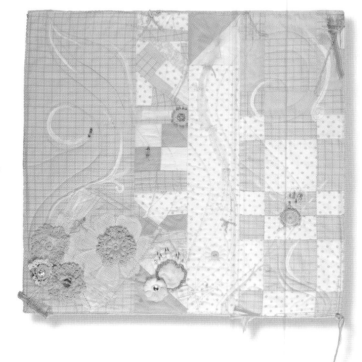

This quilt is so far from the mark when compared to my original vision for it…not better or worse, just way different. I played with a lot of techniques I don't usually use—I used paper, gesso, markers, lots of raw edges and stuff hanging off, and no binding. Some of my ideas worked well, others maybe not so much, but I learned. And overall, I liked working against the voice that said, "It won't work."

◆　◆　◆　◆　◆

Lisa Ellis
Shedding Some Light on the Block
machine appliquéd, machine quilted

A design element that I love to incorporate in my original work is rays of light. This is accomplished by defining areas just based on value. Since the antique block was yellow and white, I selected a background of purple as a perfect complement. Then I chose fabrics in the complete range of values for those three colors. The top is entirely fused and then quilted to secure the edges of each piece.

Barbara Garrett
Scraps... And More Scraps
hand and machine pieced, hand quilted

After disassembling the block, all I saw before me was a pile of yellow and white scraps. So I added more scraps, both prints and solids, in a variety of 1930s colors. Playing with different fabric combinations and drafting a variety of block patterns, I eventually turned the scraps into a collection of four-inch blocks. One of the blocks is a smaller version of the original churn dash. My love of juvenile print fabrics is evident in many of the prints I chose. I enjoyed having a reason to play with my collection of vintage 1930s scraps.

◆ ◆ ◆ ◆ ◆

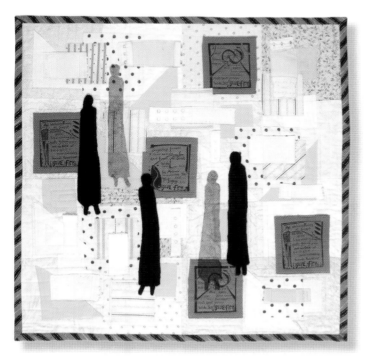

Paula Golden
Women's Lives
machine pieced, machine appliquéd, machine quilted

Who are these women, the ones whose sewing baskets get passed on to us? What do the bits and pieces left in the baskets tell us about their lives? The quilt was created to showcase a collection of bra extenders that were found in an antique sewing basket. They are paired with a favorite silhouette motif.

Judy Gula
Painted Ladies
machine pieced, machine appliquéd, machine quilted

The yellow and white block has been interspersed into the yellow block background with a pop of green. I began with vintage linens – black and white each with an embroidered grand lady who reminds me a bit of Little Bo Peep. The ladies' skirts have been trimmed with vintage hankies that feature a hand tatted edge.

◆　◆　◆　◆　◆

Mary Kerr
Eight Chicks in the Barnyard
hand and machine pieced, hand embroidered, machine quilted

The yellow and white Hole in the Barn Door block was taken apart and resewn to correct some horrible construction errors! It is surrounded by fragments of another top from that same era and penny squares that feature a pair of tiny chicks. These blocks were hand embroidered by my grandmother Say, sometime in the 1940s. She gave them to me years ago and they demanded to be used in this setting. We can all imagine the noise they could create in real life!

Kathy Lincoln
Cliffside Beach Club
machine pieced, machine quilted

There was good reason why these Churn Dash blocks were not put into a quilt! I took the block completely apart so I could use just the pieces. The yellow was a perfect match for some fabrics that I had acquired on vacation at the beach. When we vacation on Nantucket at my husband's family home, we go walking every morning, and one of the stops is the Cliffside Beach Club. From there we walk down the beach and climb forty steps to the top of the cliff. When you look down the umbrellas look like pinwheels.

◆　◆　◆　◆　◆

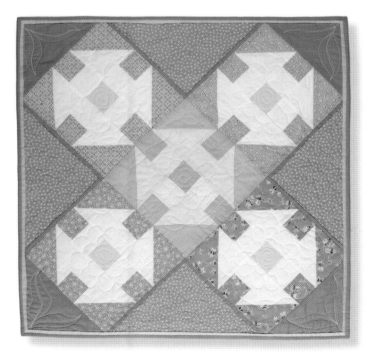

Jane Miller
Churn Dash Garden
machine pieced, machine quilted

Talk about Murphy's Law! I had to get this fourth challenge completed before the start of another school year. I looked high and low for sock monkey fabric, wanting to create the ultimate "Monkey's Wrench." But my self-imposed deadline loomed and a second thought surfaced. Shopping in my stash, the yellow fabric melded nicely with a 1950s theme of flowered prints. I created four additional blocks to surround the yellow "center," creating a larger, single pattern. Petals, leaves, and curling vines were added to soften the straight lines of the blocks. Perhaps there is a monkey hiding there after all!

Jeannie Roulet Minchak
Maine Spring Morning
machine pieced, machine quilted

I loved winter in Maine: the promise of spring as I looked out over the snow piles and roof icicles in April; the vibrant colors of blue, white, and sunshine that I saw outside my window in the morning. Soon the snow-covered gardens would be blooming with flowers - and it made everything, even mud season, seem wonderful. With this quilt, I wanted to capture the view from my window on April mornings in Maine, as I eagerly anticipated the flowers in my garden.

◆　◆　◆　◆　◆

Jeannette Muir
Carlotta
machine pieced, machine quilted

The Monkey Wrench was less of a challenge than the others because it allowed for a much wider color selection. Anything would work. The poor quality of the fabric meant that smaller pieces in the design were needed to provide support and stability. But the process of choosing the design and fabrics is always enjoyable.

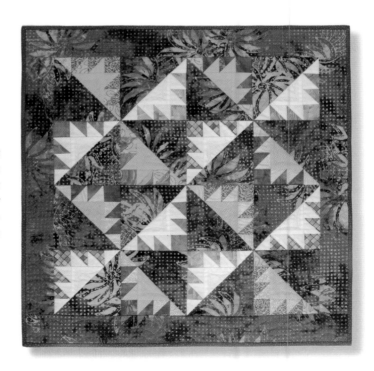

Sue Reich
In My Grandma's Day
machine pieced, machine appliquéd, machine quilted

This pattern has always reminded me of my grandmother's farmhouse in western Pennsylvania where I spent my summers growing up. It was my grandmother Martin who taught me to sew and quilt. This small quilt is a tribute to her. The printed pages were copied from a learn-to-sew book published in the 1920s, a time when my grandmother was developing her own sewing skills.

◆　◆　◆　◆　◆

Shannon Shirley
Hen and Chicks
machine pieced, hand embroidered, machine quilted

Block #4 was solid fabrics again, and I have always liked yellow, so I am not sure why I had such a problem coming up with a design for this quilt. I got frustrated one day and tossed the block down in a mess on my sewing table. The next day I noticed it was lying next to some chicken fabric I had purchased and the colors were great. My Monkey Wrench block became Hen and Chicks. The embroidery was done by hand and the wall hanging was machine quilted using a variety of methods.

Cyndi Souder
The Write Stuff
machine pieced, hand stamped, hand embellished, machine quilted

As soon as I received this block, I knew that I was going to rubber stamp on some of it. My personal challenge would be to work in the yellow/white/black palette without creating the "bumblebee" effect. I have always loved writing and I am enthralled by old writing implements. These artifacts came from my grandmother's desk at her farmhouse. I can only imagine the correspondence, the lists, and the ledgers these pens have touched. This quilt arose from a timely unearthing of the pens and the happy discovery of these stamps in my collection.

◆　◆　◆　◆　◆

Pam Weeks
Churn Dash Monochrome
machine pieced, machine quilted

In 1995 I was blessed with a five-day workshop with Nancy Crow. We were challenged in many ways to work outside our boundaries, and what I came away with was a desire to incorporate traditional patchwork with my love of color and playfulness. We were directed to turn our cutting boards over so the lines weren't there and to put away our rulers. Nancy taught us to cut and piece spontaneously, and I learned to honor the patterns while playing with color and value. This challenge block was so weirdly pieced that it begged to be deconstructed and played with, so play I did!

Mary Kerr
A Crooked Barn
machine pieced, machine appliquéd, machine quilted by
Linda Hahn, 52x52 inches

Whether you choose to call these blocks Monkey Wrench, Churn Dash, or Hole in the Barn Door, they were a mess! No two were the same size and the fabric was of poor quality. The remaining 16 blocks were definitely the worst of the lot! They were incorporated into this quilt I call, A Crooked Barn. I embraced the wonkiness of the blocks and chose to ignore the loss of points in each motif. The blocks were embellished with equally wonky appliqué pieces from the same era. I purposely left the crooked lines and the basting stitches. The backing is a bright feedsack and it was bound with fabric from my grandmother Wilson.

*T*he blocks for the fifth round of quilts came from a set of twenty blocks that were once part of a damaged quilt top. The top had been disassembled before I rescued it, and most of the poorly executed appliqué blocks had seen better days. The motifs were machine appliquéd and some of the blocks had pieces missing. The original maker of this quilt seemed to have far more vision than skill!

The appliqué block presented design challenges for some of our artists. Jeannette Muir and Bonnie Dwyer both told me that this was the hardest block to work with. As always, there was rarely consensus in the ranks.

Jane Miller disagreed, saying, "This is probably my favorite block of the set. I had fun finding fabrics to complement the colors of the original appliqué. And, while I wasn't the most experienced quilter in the group, I felt I could hold my head high among them! I was certainly growing as a quilter AND a person!!"

The blocks were sent out just after the debut of the first 80 quilts at The Mid-Atlantic Quilt Festival in February 2008. Those of us who were able to attend MAQF were energized by the comments, excitement, and curiosity of the viewers. I was in awe just watching others respond to our collection. We knew our project was special, but the validation of the quilting public was a giant energy boost.

Doris Bloomer spoke for many of us when she said, "This project has really stretched me and definitely put me outside of my box. It has given me greater confidence in my abilities to deal with patterns and blocks to design what I was picturing in my head. Before I strictly worked with a given pattern but now I feel I can design my own quilt just the way I want it."

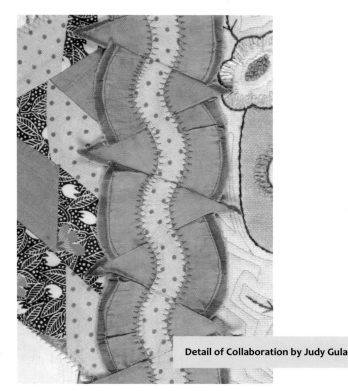

Detail of Collaboration by Judy Gula

Detail of For My Sister by Doris Bloomer

The Fifth Set of Quilts

Doris Bloomer
For My Sister
hand and machine pieced, hand appliquéd, hand quilted

Cancer has touched my life in so many ways over my lifetime. I have lost my parents, my grandmother, and a very dear friend to this dreadful disease. Now it has claimed my sister-in-law who died this year of brain cancer. This little quilt is just a way to remember her. I picked the Seven Sisters block as a focal point, and the colors because they remind me of her. She loved happy colors and would be thrilled to know that, even after she is gone, I'm still making quilts for her.

Linda Cooper
Great Aunt Augusta
hand and machine appliquéd, hand inked, machine quilted

I've tried with each of these challenges to push my quilting efforts beyond what I've done before. My great-aunt, Augusta Geiger, was a beautiful woman who died in her twenties of an infected toe. I used Tsukineko inks on my hand-dyed fabric to create her face. I totally enjoyed making her outfit and hat (the challenge pieces are on the hat band). The original photos are fabric-transferred on the back of the quilt, and show Augusta and her sister, Hedwig, who was a milliner, in my hometown of Piqua, Ohio.

Karen Dever
My Rose Garden
machine pieced, hand appliquéd, machine quilted

Using the style of the original block, I created, "My Rose Garden," with vintage and new fabric. The original block was completely taken apart and reused. Can you find the original fabric?

◆　◆　◆　◆　◆

Bonnie Dwyer
Keep it Simple
machine pieced, machine appliquéd, machine quilted

With this quilt, I continue on the quilting journey of trying new techniques. Other than re-minding me of lollipops, this block really stumped me. So I resorted to the "keep it simple" principle. Instead of putting effort into redesigning it, I decided to make the most of the original block and focus on machine quilting. I used some echo, free-form meandering, as well as a few embroi-dery stitches built into the machine. This was so much fun!

Lori East
Redneck Girls
machine pieced, machine appliquéd, hand embellished, machine quilted

Redneck Girls represents a jumble of happy memories. The song reminds me of a mini-roadtrip in 2002 when Pam Weeks and Mary Kerr and I drove from Vermont to New Hampshire and back. The photo brings Teddy Pruett to mind….antiquing with her in Florida. In both cases, I remember laughing—a lot. As I worked, I thought of the girls in the photo, how tickled they seem to be. I thought of many little Dale Evans wannabes too, how they yearned for a shiny pair of red cowgirl boots. And I thought of all the real redneck girls I know.

Lisa Ellis
Connecting the Dots
fused fabric technique, machine appliquéd, machine quilted

Who am I? I am different things to different people. I have many faces. I'd like to connect the dots to understand my real self. How did I become so many people? Where is my true self headed in the future? Am I authentic? Am I true to my beliefs? Who knows the real me? I think I know the answer to the last one.

Barbara Garrett
Faded Glory
hand and machine pieced, machine appliquéd, hand quilted

What happens as a quilt ages? Its colors mellow and mingle, with perhaps a bit of fading. Some age staining appears. It acquires an overall age patina that says, "I'm comfortable with what I've become." Throughout this entire project, a personal challenge of mine was to work with fabric from the same time period as the fabric in each challenge block. It was a bit more of a struggle to find fabric for this quilt, as I wished to impart some remembered glory to a faded quilt block, while maintaining the block's integrity. I'm pleased with the results.

◆　　◆　　◆　　◆　　◆

Paula Golden
Prisms
machine pieced, hand appliquéd, hand embellished, machine quilted

Rainbows dance and light laughs across the kitchen floor as the sunlight is reflected through antique chandelier prisms. Pieces of this block were altered by fabric ink and accented with glass beads.

Judy Gula
Collaboration
machine pieced, machine appliquéd, hand embellished, machine quilted

It has nothing to do with the fabrics and everything to do with the process. This quilt was designed while attending a quilt retreat. It truly was a collaboration of many quilters. The original block can be seen in the basket and ribbon. The flower arrangement is vintage embroidery. Also included are vintage fabrics and trims.

◆　◆　◆　◆　◆

Mary Kerr
A Faded Memory
hand and machine pieced, machine appliquéd, machine quilted

With this quilt, I challenged myself to use period-appropriate fabrics in an equal state of disrepair. The block I was working with had suffered extensive damage along its stem and only half of the flower was able to be salvaged. I paired it with another faded block from the 1880s and bordered it with a fugitive purple calico whose color has faded to brown. The backing is a fragment of a cheater cloth from the same era. I was further challenged as the fabrics continued to shatter during the quilting process, adding even more holes and character spots.

Kathy Lincoln
1901
machine pieced, machine quilted

The block had been on my design wall sneering at me for months. Finally, I had a breakthrough moment (at least I hope so since I had commenced cutting and sewing). I had been looking through books of public domain blocks and I found one called, "Arabic Lattice." The pieces in it would accommodate the pieces for the disassembled block, and I liked the look of the block. I did some more research and found out the block was first published in 1901. That is approximately the time of the original block so it seemed a perfect match.

◆　　◆　　◆　　◆　　◆

Jane Miller
Vintage Rose
machine pieced, machine appliquéd, machine quilted

Oh sweet Vintage Rose. As I studied the fifth block, I began to ask questions: Where did it come from? What were the original plans? How many blocks were there going to be? Was it an original pattern? What happened to its creator? Of course, I can only imagine the answers to all these questions, and will never really know. But happily, the block is now finished and ready for display, and at least temporarily, reunited with its friends. What questions do you have?

Jeannie Roulet Minchak
Even Quilt Girls Get the Blues
machine pieced, hand embellished, machine quilted

The fun part of the Vintage Revisited project has been letting the blocks tell me what they want, and not the other way around. When I first saw this block, it said comfy old jeans, dusty cattle farms, and hot summer evenings with loved ones on the porch - the reassurance of the old, the excitement of the new, and the sadness when things we love change.

◆　◆　◆　◆　◆

Jeannette Muir
Francis Eunice
machine pieced, machine appliquéd, machine quilted

Not being good at appliqué, this block really threw me for a loop. It was the ugliest one so far. Should I attempt to make it beautiful or make it uglier? I lost some sleep over this one. Of course, like all the others, I picked it all apart. Then I soaked the badly-stained background fabric for three hours in Oxyclean© and ironed it onto freezer paper. I then scanned four new batiks onto the old fabric. The viewer can decide whether it is better or worse.

Sue Reich
Vintage Enshrined
machine pieced, machine appliquéd, hand embellished, hand quilted

This machine-appliquéd flower was a very enjoyable block to redesign. The lace and the white fabrics with tucks were once a beautiful, antique pillowcase purchased in Connecticut. The white fabric was very fragile. I was able to salvage enough for a flower pot. The lace formed a double border on the case and provided just enough to enshrine this lovely flower.

◆　◆　◆　◆　◆

Shannon Shirley
Chelsea's Bouquet
machine pieced, hand appliquéd, hand embellished, machine quilted

The background fabric from the original block is used on the back as a label. I hand blanket-stitched the vintage appliqué and the new pieces onto the new background. This piece was free-motion quilted and embellished with beads before the backing was put on. The fabric used is a selection from Moda's collection, Chelsea's Boutique.

Cyndi Souder
Circling the Drain
machine pieced, machine appliquéd, hand embellished, machine quilted

This block was absolutely the biggest challenge so far. The design, the colors... nothing appealed to me. I joked that this block was so awful that it was circling the drain. And once I said that, I couldn't get that image out of my brain! I took the block apart, added fusible under some of the fabric, and played with what it would look like if the pieces actually were circling the drain. As with some of the other quilts in this series, I stamped some of the fabric and depended on fusible for a lot of the construction.

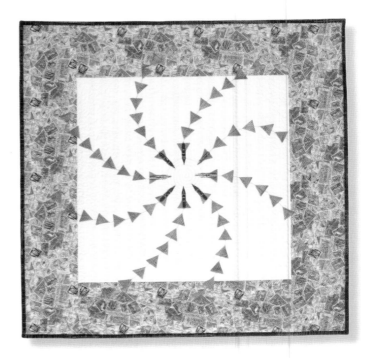

◆ ◆ ◆ ◆ ◆

Pam Weeks
Brown Rose by Any Other Name
hand and machine pieced, machine appliquéd, machine quilted

Color drives the composition in my quilts and when I'm working successfully, tradition mixes with color play and the works sing with history and hue. Nature inspires me. If one looks carefully at the world, one finds amazing contrasts and combinations of colors within a field, tree, or river. Light plays on leaves or water and reflects other colors. All things, all colors, all traditions influence my work–I am bound by none.

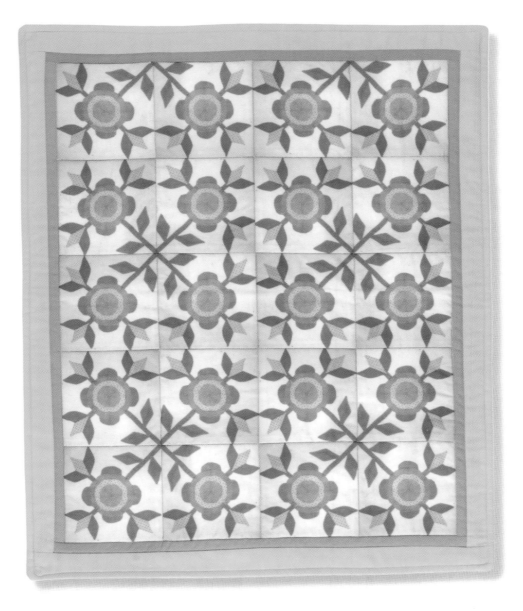

Mary Kerr
In Its Glory
machine pieced, machine quilted, 18x22 inches

    The blocks for this challenge came from a faded set of 20 poorly executed floral blocks from about 1900. I photographed the best block and printed 20 miniature blocks onto photo transfer paper to give the viewer an idea of what this maker may have intended her finished quilt to look like. In its glory, it would have been lovely!

This final letter to my ladies was out of the norm. When they opened the package containing block #6, they read:

"Enclosed is the last of our six 'blocks.' This one is a bit different in that it is a fragment of a vintage Grandmother's Flower Garden top from the 1940s. Many of you know that the Flower Garden is my favorite pattern and it is an integral part of many (most) of my pieces. Thank you for allowing me to insert my preferences once again as I invite you to play! You are each receiving a 12-16 inch piece of this quilt top."

The responses to the fragments were as varied as with other blocks. Some were thrilled to work with the colors of the 1940s and others were left shaking their heads.

Cindi Souder said, "When I agreed to participate in Vintage Revisited, I did it for Mary. I felt honored to be invited and I wanted to help her out with this project, but I don't do vintage. When each block arrived, I thought it was worse – um, I mean more challenging – than the last. The teal and cheddar was hard. The red, white, and blue screamed flag to me; I'm patriotic, but I don't make patriotic quilts. By the time the Grandmother's Flower Garden fragment arrived, I thought I'd lose my mind."

As the final quilts began to arrive in my mailbox, I found myself completely overwhelmed. The group had astounded me all along but their efforts this round left me breathless. They all seemed to save their best for last. Each of the quilts has my name in the title, which I thought was an interesting coincidence, and I was very touched. Only later did they fill me in on the "real" story.

Jeannie Minchak explains, "For the last quilt, a scrap of a Grandmother's Flower Garden, one of the quilt artists sent out an e-mail asking if we wouldn't mind naming our finished quilts after Mary in gratitude for being asked to work on this project. The response was an overwhelming YES! I never found out what happened when Mary finally "caught on" to what we'd done, but I chuckled while creating my quilt thinking what Mary's reaction would be."

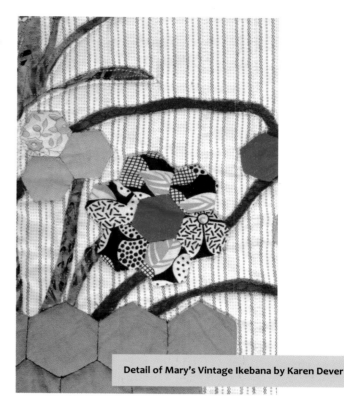

Detail of Mary's Vintage Ikebana by Karen Dever

Detail of Mary, Mary, Uncontrary by Sue Reich

Doris Bloomer
Going on a Trip with Mary...
machine pieced, hand quilted

This little quilt concludes the "trip" I have taken with Mary. How much fun this has been, and what a challenge! I definitely had to think outside the box on many of the quilt blocks. I am a fairly traditional quilter and usually make my quilts based on patterns found in books and magazines. To design something out of the blue was very unusual and stretched my mind quite a bit. This challenge also enabled me to try out several patterns I had been meaning to make on a smaller scale. Thank you, Mary, for being patient with me when I didn't meet the deadline and for letting me participate in this wonderful adventure.

◆　◆　◆　◆　◆

Linda Cooper
Mary's Quilt Show
hand and machine pieced, machine appliquéd, machine quilted

I took a picture of hex paper on an angle, and paper-pieced the perspective Grandmother's Flower Garden block from the one Mary gave us. I printed pictures of the first four challenges and arranged those on poster board and shot those pictures in perspective. Then I printed sections of the quilts on fabric to make the outdoor quilt show. I had the top half of Mary (taken by Cyndi Souder) hanging a quilt and took the rest of her body from an internet image. I thank all the challenge quilt makers for permission to use their quilt images. Thanks for the fun, Mary!

Karen Dever
Mary's Vintage Ikebana
machine pieced, hand appliquéd, machine quilted

As someone who does not work with early 20^{th-} century fabrics, this chunk of a quilt presented me with a dilemma. How do I use these fabrics in a contemporary fashion? If you have seen my previous creations you see my fondness for garden inspiration, so adding batiks to the design brings this design into the 21st-century.

◆　◆　◆　◆　◆

Bonnie Dwyer
Proud Mary
hand and machine pieced, machine appliquéd, machine quilted

This final quilt in the block challenge is a tribute to Mary Kerr, who not only had the idea but also pursued it! Mary's favorite color is orange and her favorite vintage block is the Grandmother's Flower Garden, so I combined the two in this version of a flower garden, complete with a white picket fence.

Lori East

I Don't Think We're in Kansas Anymore, Mary
hand and machine pieced, hand appliquéd, hand embellished, hand embroidered, machine quilted

When I first met Mary, one of the first things we found we had in common was that we had both lived in Kansas. That was at the Vermont Quilt Festival, in 2002, and in just a few days' time all of us who would become the Lost Girls, Mary, Pam Weeks, Sue Reich, Bonnie Dwyer, Kathy Metelica, and I, became friends. I have been so blessed by my friendship with these women, in spite of all the many changes that our lives have undergone and the distances between us. We always have a blast together, but no matter where we are, I'm pretty sure it's not Kansas.

◆   ◆   ◆   ◆   ◆

Lisa Ellis

Mary's Heroes
hand and machine pieced, machine appliquéd, machine quilted

This piece is dedicated to Mary Kerr as thanks for her inspiration and vision for creating this amazing quilt project. The Grandmother's Flower Garden block brings thoughts about the importance and influence of the elder women in our lives. I love how Mary Kerr celebrates these relationships on her website on her Heroes page. I wanted to celebrate these women and create a memento for Mary. So, thank you, Mary, for including me in Vintage Revisited. It's been tremendously rewarding.

Barbara Garrett
Mary, Mary... How Does Your Garden Grow?
hand and machine pieced, hand quilted

    I knew the moment I saw the Grandmother's Flower Garden quilt fragment that I had the perfect circa 1920s garden-scene cretonne to complement it. The colors blended perfectly, and the girl watering her flower garden with all her woodland friends made an ideal center for the medallion style quilt.

◆   ◆   ◆   ◆   ◆

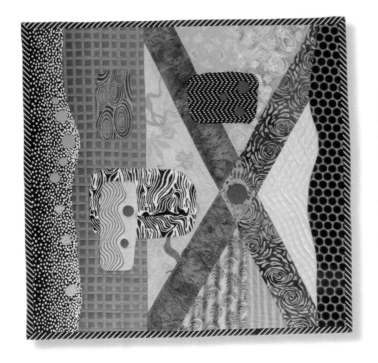

Paula Golden
Hugs and Kisses to Mary
machine pieced, hand and machine appliquéd, machine quilted

    It is a joy to be part of the quilting tradition. Pieces of the Grandmother's Flower Garden block were appliquéd to an exuberant background of pieced fabrics.

Judy Gula
To Mary, You Are Loved
hand and machine pieced, hand embellished, hand embroidered, machine quilted

I thought this embroidery was perfect for the last quilt in this series. The embroidery has the following saying: "To love and be loved is the greatest joy in the earth." The Grandmother's Flower Garden block is easily recognized in the border, and is accented with vintage trim and motifs. The blue birds have been beaded. This quilt is a tribute to Mary who had the vision, encouragement, and perseverance to bring Vintage Revisited to life.

◆ ◆ ◆ ◆ ◆

Mary Kerr
My Memories of Minnie
hand and machine pieced, hand embellished, hand embroidered, machine quilted

This quilt is one of my collage quilts that serves to showcase family memorabilia. The base fabrics were a fragment of a top from the 1940s that I paired with the scraps of Grandmother's Flower Garden. To this I added articles that came from my grandmother, Minnie Opal Wilson's (1912–2007), estate. Included is a baby jacket that my father wore, a tiny silver ring, belt buckles, sewing items and buttons –- always buttons!

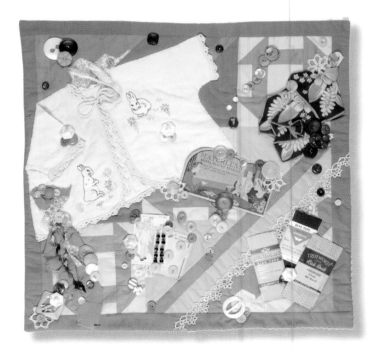

Kathy Lincoln
My Favorite "Maryism"
hand and machine pieced, machine appliquéd, machine quilted

Mary uses this quote frequently and I just love it. The quote came to mind when I was looking at the piece of Grandma's Flower Garden quilt top she had given me. The blocks looked like flowered panties so I had to follow the block's instructions and make this quilt.

◆   ◆   ◆   ◆   ◆

Jane Miller
A View for Mary
hand and machine pieced, machine quilted

The Flower Garden blocks peek out from an Attic Windows setting. The old is mixed with the new to provide a new and exciting view of quilting possibilities. Vintage Revisited has given me the opportunity to look at my quilting in a whole new light.

Jeannie Roulet Minchak
The Friends in Mary's Garden
hand and machine pieced, hand appliquéd, machine quilted

I wanted to do something different with the traditional Grandmother's Flower Garden design, and yet retain the design's hexagon theme as homage to Mary Kerr who loves it. This quilt is the result: 20 paper-pieced hexagon "flowers" are planted in the center garden to honor Mary and the other talented quilters I had the pleasure to be associated with on this project. The cardinals in the corner represent the State of Virginia (where Mary and I have lived) and the bluebirds are my wish for happiness to all involved.

◆　◆　◆　◆　◆

Jeannette Muir
Mary's Garden - Deployed
hand and machine pieced, machine quilted

What great fun this was... The solution finally came to me in the middle of the night, a nightmare, actually. Instead of picking apart, as I usually do, I simply cut it apart and put it back together again. The best garden I have ever had. What could be easier? "Digging" in my fabric stash is always fun. No weeding, no watering. Grandma would be proud!

Sue Reich
Mary, Mary, Uncontrary, Watching Her Quilt Garden Grow!
hand and machine pieced, hand appliquéd, machine quilted

I wanted to showcase Mary's love of this pattern, her friends, and our deep connection. The quilts and friends in Mary's garden provide a safe, serene place to enjoy the colors and contemplate the possibilities!

◆　◆　◆　◆　◆

Shannon Shirley
M is for Mary
hand and machine pieced, machine appliquéd, hand embellished, hand embroidered, machine quilted

I received this block after returning from a trip to Lancaster Pennsylvania. While in Lancaster, I had stopped at an antique store and purchased a few things, which included a dresser scarf with hummingbirds on it. Well, as you can see, part of that dresser scarf became part of my quilt because the colors were perfect with my section of the Grandmothers Flower Garden quilt top.

Cyndi Souder
To Mary, Who Has Kept Us All Rolling Along
machine pieced, machine appliquéd, hand
stamped, machine quilted

From the moment I saw this photograph of
my husband adjusting his bicycle wheel on a Boy
Scout trip (thanks to Bill Branner for permission
to use the image), I knew it was destined to be a
quilt. Since I knew I had a deadline for this final
quilt in the Vintage Revisited series, I decided that
the time constraint would motivate me to get this
done. I had a love-hate relationship with this quilt
throughout the process as I allowed it to guide me
rather than the other way around. I blogged about
the process and that made the experience more
meaningful and productive.

◆　◆　◆　◆　◆

Pam Weeks
So, Mary!!
hand and machine pieced, machine quilted

I absolutely hate Grandmother's Flower Garden quilts! Perhaps it's because my grandmother's
garden was so lovely, and these quilts pale in
comparison. Maybe it's the Nile green. When I
opened the envelope from Mary, I nearly choked.
The block stayed on my design wall for months and
every time I looked at it, I saw red. Then I started
seeing orange and purple, and I knew it was time
to start cutting. It wasn't until I was nearly done
that I saw I had chosen the same colors as in the
block. Same colors, different values.

Mary Kerr
My Boys of Edisto
hand and machine pieced, machine embroidered, machine
quilted by Shannon Shirley, 34x34 inches

   The "blocks" for this challenge came from a battered
quilt top from about 1940. I paired the remaining fragments
with blocks from the 1880s and a 1950s embroidered piece
that was initially destined to become an apron front. This
embroidery honors my two musical sons, Sean and Ryan,
and our family love of Edisto Island, South Carolina.

Detail of Redneck Girls by Lori East

Additional Thoughts from the Artists

I started the whole thing as kind of a lark and was astonished at the places I went with it. Those places may not be evident in my work, but they are very real in my confidence and attitude. I have learned that I am not an artist, I am a rule-breaker. Tell me I can't and I will, just to prove you wrong...but only if I really want to.

Lori East

Detail of It's About Time by Cyndi Souder

While working on this project, I felt a connection with the quiltmaker who had made the antique block...wondering who she (he?!) was, what prompted her to make it, why it never got finished. I was constantly astounded at why certain quiltmakers used certain techniques in their blocks, and felt as if they were teaching me through the years. Then as I completed my work, I felt a huge connection with the other 19 quilt artists working on this project, knowing we all were using the same block and knowing each of us was doing something totally different. It is a huge circle of creativity spanning the years.

Jeannie Minchak

I love the progression you can see when you look at all six rounds in order. In the beginning, we were all so timid. Then we saw what everyone else did to that first block and we pushed the next block a little further. Each round showed new artistic courage, new boundaries. By the end, everyone threw caution to the wind and did what they wanted to do. It was a blast! I started out thinking that this was just another challenge. In the end, this project changed the course of my quilting. I pushed, I learned, and I grew as a quilter. I'm so glad I had the chance to participate.

Cyndi Souder

Oh, what a journey it was!

Jane Miller

Detail of A View for Mary by Jane Miller

Now that you have seen this unique collection of quilts, I hope you are inspired to organize your own challenge. This type of project provides an opportunity for quilters of all skills, disciplines and traditions to participate. Vintage Revisited has several artists who considered themselves to be beginning quilters. We have award winning artists, authors and teachers. We have quilters who have never chosen to show their work on a public stage prior to these exhibits. All were able to be equal participants in the process.

Who is in charge?

The first step is to determine who is in charge. A bossy "Type A" works best when they are the one calling the shots. Co-coordinators are able to share the decisions and direct with a united front. Some groups like to give all their members an equal opportunity to contribute.

I was the sole coordinator and decision maker for *Vintage Revisited*. It worked for us because I took complete ownership of the project. I established the guidelines, including size requirements and which blocks would be used. The participants knew the rules coming into the project and could focus on the design process without the distraction of details. I had full responsibility for the schedule, travel dates and future exhibits.

Some would not feel comfortable with this dictatorial approach and might work best with a committee. From past experience with many groups, small is best when decisions need to be made.

Define Your Group

Second, you will need to define your group. How many participants do you want to work with? How many blocks do you have to distribute? I initially thought I would work with 12 artists and had several sets of blocks in mind. When the group was formed with the perfect 19, I had to dig for larger block sets.

If you are planning to exhibit the quilts, you may want to limit the number to a manageable size. How many quilts can your local show accommodate? There are 117 quilts in *Vintage Revisited,* and very few shows have space to exhibit them all at one time. I separated the sets and many venues chose to display part in one year and the rest in another.

Detail of High in the Sky by Sue Reich

Deciding who can participate is easier if you working with a guild or an already established group. I encourage you to include a wide range of talents and traditions. What makes this project so exciting is that we all bring different skills, traditions and voices to the table.

Set Deadlines

Set a deadline for acceptance. Decide how you are going to handle participants who may have to drop out. Will they be required to return the blocks? Does your group plan to accept late comers to the party? There will be people who ask to join once they see how much fun you are having. All these issues are likely to come up and it will be easier to deal with them if you plan ahead. When one of my artists was not able to finish the last three quilts, I did not consider replacing her. I simply adjusted the final numbers. Her work is an integral part of the first three sets and her support for the project has been unfailing.

Set a firm due date but be willing to compromise. I had a set schedule that listed when each quilt was due. We had four months to complete each quilt. Knowing how deadlines often work, I allowed time for shipping, photography, labels, and life's interruptions. I had said from the beginning that this was to be a project that made our hearts sing. Creating these quilts was to be a challenge, not a stressful exercise.

A few of my artists were never late. Others asked for a little extra time. Still others waited until I published the "drop dead" date to complete and send me their quilts. I finished several of my own quilts at the last minute and frequently asked for quilting help. We began exhibiting the first sets quilts before the project was finished. Various show and photography deadlines provided an excellent incentive to finish.

Vintage Revisited was an ambitious project. We had 19 busy women who experienced a wide range of challenges over the course of this two-year endeavor. The roller coaster of emotions is mind boggling. Together we lost loved ones, sent children to college, battled cancer, moved multiple times, started new jobs, donated a kidney, welcomed grandchildren, and planned a wedding. It is amazing to me that we finished 117 quilts.

Who cares if some deadlines were adjusted?

Establish the Rules and Put Them in Writing

Every successful project has a shared set of guidelines. Each member needs to understand what the parameters of the project encompass. Vintage revisited had three simple rules: use the vintage block in your finished quilt, make it 24 x 24, and have fun!

These are the rules that worked for us, but there is an endless list of options you may want to consider. Whatever you decide, put the rules and the deadlines in writing and make sure every member of your group has a copy. Repeat them often with a smile. Be prepared to adjust your expectations as needed. One of my artists rechecked my first letter as she was preparing to send her quilt. She was horrified to discover that her quilt would be considerably larger than the rest. I refused her offer to remake this gorgeous quilt and it hangs proudly with its smaller relatives.

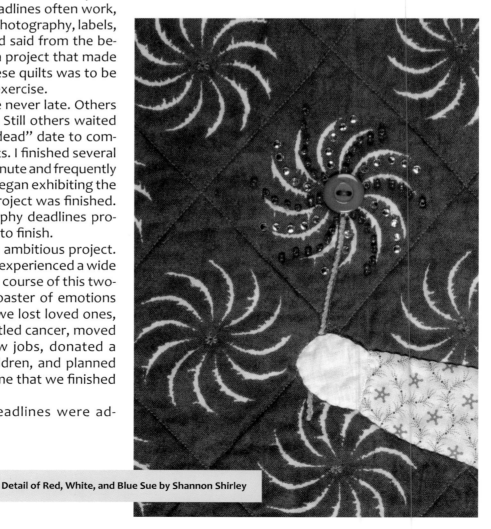

Detail of Red, White, and Blue Sue by Shannon Shirley

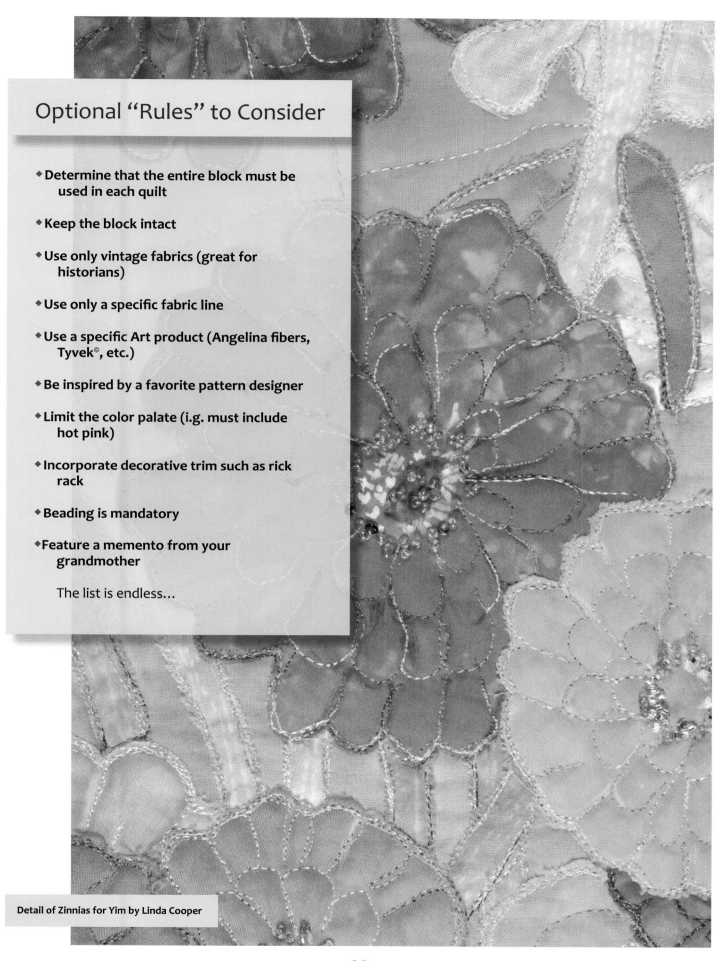

Optional "Rules" to Consider

- Determine that the entire block must be used in each quilt

- Keep the block intact

- Use only vintage fabrics (great for historians)

- Use only a specific fabric line

- Use a specific Art product (Angelina fibers, Tyvek©, etc.)

- Be inspired by a favorite pattern designer

- Limit the color palate (i.g. must include hot pink)

- Incorporate decorative trim such as rick rack

- Beading is mandatory

- Feature a memento from your grandmother

    The list is endless...

Detail of Zinnias for Yim by Linda Cooper

VARIATIONS·ON THE·THEME

Star Blocks, c.1940

Personal Challenge

Who says you always have to play with others? See what happens if you take a set of blocks and complete it in a variety of ways. You can choose any block, any size, and any number of variations. You only have to make yourself happy.

I took four pink and white star blocks and created the four small art quilts you see here. I kept the size to a diminutive 11 inches square and loved the exercise in "thinking small." These were created during a retreat when I was trying to teach myself to machine quilt. I have since determined that I quilt best by check!

Edisto by Mary Kerr, 2006

Duo Challenges

What happens if you share blocks with a friend? A set of blocks? Perhaps you want to split a set of blocks with several close friends. Maybe you have twenty blocks that you plan to share with 4-5 others.

The small group challenges are wonderful but they tend to be loosely organized and are often set up without deadlines. I have numerous sets that I have shared with friends that are in the "some day I'll finish that" category. We often put off those things that do not have a determined deadline. Be sure to set tentative rules if completion is your goal.

Pretty in Pink by Mary Kerr, 2006

Happy Hour by Mary Kerr, 2006

Tropical Smoothie by Mary Kerr, 2006

One Block Challenge with Extras

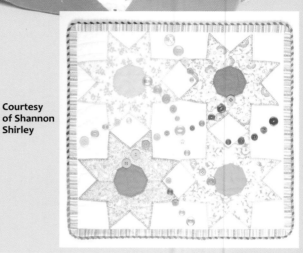

In 2007, I issued a challenge to one of my business groups. The Quilters Professional Network is a talented group of professional quilters from the Mid-Atlantic States who convene for an annual conference and educational seminar each March.

Several of the members are also Vintage Revisited participants and all have been overwhelmingly supportive of the project. I was curious to see what would be produced if the project was a one quilt commitment.

I gave them each a packet of materials that included a 1930s star block, vintage rick rack and a variety of buttons. Each of the participants received an identical packet. They were given one year to complete the 18x18 inch quilt and were encouraged to use all the products in their packets.

I loved the addition of embellishments and felt that the extra challenge added a new dimension to the project. Some of the finished quilts are shown here.

Imagine if you based a challenge around a unique set of vintage buttons or treasured trim from your grandmother's sewing basket. What if each participant were provided with a vintage dresser scarf, handkerchief, or an antique button card? Again, the possibilities are endless.

Courtesy of Shannon Shirley

Courtesy of Kathleen Davies

Courtesy of Mary Kerr

Courtesy of BJ Titus

Courtesy of Mary Ann Ciccotelli

Courtesy of Didi Salvatierra

Courtesy of Kim Morris

Courtesy of Karen Dever

Courtesy of Jane Hamilton

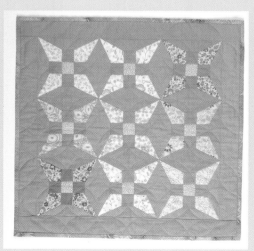

Courtesy of Jeannette Muir

One Block Challenge

In 2008, I challenged this group of quilt professionals for a second time. I gave them this yellow and white block, circa 1940, entitled Roosevelt and asked each of the participants to create a small 12 x 12 inch quilt. They were asked to bring their finished pieces to the next year's conference in March 2009. Some of the quilts from this one block challenge are shown here.

Courtesy of Jeannette Muir

Courtesy of BJ Titus

Courtesy of Cher Hurney

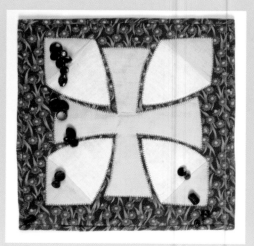

Courtesy of Mary Kerr

Courtesy of Shannon Shirley

Courtesy of Kathy Lincoln

Courtesy of Karen Dever

Courtesy of Kathleen Davies

Courtesy of Mary Ann Ciccotelli

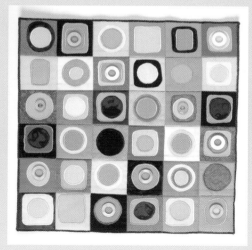

Courtesy of Didi Salvatierra

Go Big

The beauty of this project is that anyone in your group can participate and enjoy creating in his or her own unique style. Art quilters can create art quilts; traditionalists can enjoy their favorite fabrics; historians can play with their vintage scraps. Everyone can create a piece that makes their own heart sing.

What happens if you decide to Go Big? What if you increase the number of participants? 30 ladies from your guild? 50 of your internet buddies? 75 assorted blocks from the 1930s? 100 different Dresden Plate blocks? Just imagine what you can dream up next!

Non-Vintage Block Ideas

I focused on vintage blocks because that is what I love. I chose the patterns and fabrics I was familiar with and raided my stash for sets of blocks. Each of the six sets of blocks used in Vintage Revisited came from my own collection of vintage textiles.

What doors open if we expand the project to non-vintage pieces? Think of the unfinished projects we all have in our workrooms. The quilt you started with the intention of hand piecing 80 stars stalled at 22 blocks. You may no longer be interested in finishing your masterpiece but think of the fun you could have sharing these orphans with 21 friends. Together you could create a collection of 22 quilts inspired by your star blocks.

No unfinished projects? Encourage your group to each make a _____ block (fill in your favorite pattern). Exchange the blocks (or not) and ask each member to create a small quilt using the block they received. This could be problematic if participants are not comfortable altering another's work or if they are particularly attached to their original block. The rules can be adjusted to accommodate the sentiments of each group.

What's Next?

I have only scratched the surface of possible combinations and potential projects. I would love to hear what you come up with. Please send me your story with some pictures. Together we will see what happens next.

Set of Star Blocks, c 1890

Set of small Basket Blocks, c 1880

Choosing the Blocks

There are a number of issues that should be considered before you work with vintage blocks. Many of these pieces were left undone for good reason. Vintage blocks are not for the perfectionist quilter. We have to understand that the sensibilities of past eras are not necessarily our own.

Poor quality fabrics can distort the finished size, causing the block to stretch or pull out of shape. If the block does not lay flat on your worktable, it may bow in your finished project unless you take care to correct the problems. Thin fabrics can be reinforced with interfacing or another layer of cotton. Some of the Vintage Revisited artists used fusible web for their appliqué designs.

Many blocks were not finished because of inferior workmanship. Check the seam allowances to insure that the pieces will not separate as they are pressed and sewn into a new project. If there is not a quarter inch around the outside of the design, you may lose points and the overall image will be distorted. Many of the blocks we work with are not square and vary in size. Some of us are not bothered by these issues and others prefer to remake the offending blocks.

Detail of Night Flight by Barbara Garrett

Dirt and Stains

Each of us has our own comfort level when we address the issue of dirt and stains. I see most stains as well deserved age spots and freckles, but I do prefer to work with clean fabric. If you are bothered by the condition of your block, please take the time to wash it before you start playing with it. Yes, it may fall apart, but most blocks do well if they are gently hand washed. If it is going to have issues, I would rather realize this at the start. A gentle soak in a good quality quilt wash (there are many on the market) will remove surface dirt and some stains. Restoration© is the best product for removing overall yellowing. Do not put your blocks in the washing machine and follow the manufacturer's directions.

Old fashioned Safguard soap will get smoke smells out of vintage textiles. Unwrap a bar of white soap, wrap it in a white paper towel, and place the soap and offending blocks in a sealed plastic bag for two or three days. Repeat as needed until the odor is removed. The bar of soap can be used in this way indefinitely.

Dissecting the Block

If you choose to take your block apart, a good ripper is your best friend. The goal is to save as much material as possible so you can use the block's fabric in a new and exciting way. For both hand and machine stitched seams, gently remove the stitches from the underside of the fabric by snipping every other thread. You do not want to try to rip the seam or pull a long thread. Both of these methods will distort the fabric.

Tips to Remember

♦ Crooked settings camouflage uneven block sizes

♦ Vintage and contemporary fabrics mix well

♦ It is okay to combine vintage fabrics from multiple eras

♦ Vintage fabric responds well to being stamped or overdyed

♦ Embellishments can be used cover a multitude of flaws

♦ Ignore the quilt police – they are not invited to this party

♦ Give yourself permission to play

♦ Relax, enjoy, and create what makes your heart sing!

Cheers For the Red, White and Blue by Mary Kerr

Balls in the Air by Lisa Ellis

Detail of Arabelle by Jeannette Muir

INTRODUCING·THE·ARTISTS

Doris Bloomer
Appling, Georgia

Doris grew up in Mainz, Germany, and became an American citizen in 2006 (after 25 years as an Army wife). She has been quilting for almost twenty years and loves hand quilting. She and her husband have four children, three of whom have followed their father's footsteps into the military.

Linda Cooper
Burke, Virginia
www.lindacooperquilts.com

Linda loves all aspects of the quilt world but has gravitated to art quilting in the past few years. She currently teaches fabric painting and raw-edge appliqué classes. She has a quilt travelling with Ami Simms, *Alzheimer's: Forgetting Piece by Piece* exhibit; another on permanent display at Walter Reed Army Hospital; and a third in RaNae Merrill's 2008 book, *Simply Amazing Spiral Quilts*.

Karen Dever
Moorestown, New Jersey
www.karendever.com

Karen is a retired elementary school teacher who has been involved with the quilt world for over twenty years. She is an award winning quilter and designer who is also an American Quilters' Society certified quilt appraiser. She collects antique and vintage textiles as inspiration for her lectures, workshops, and designs. Karen divides her time among quilting, traveling with her husband, and her grandchildren, who live nearby.

Bonnie Dwyer
Manchester, Maine
www.bonniedwyer.com

Bonnie has been involved and intrigued with textiles since learning to sew at an early age. She first sewed garments for her dolls, then for herself, and then for her family. She then developed an interest in quilting during the mid-1980s and went on to study quilt making, quilt history, and quilt appraising. She became certified as an appraiser by the American Quilters' Society in 2006.

Lori East
Carthage, Missouri

Lori is a quilt artist and historian who is also an American Quilters' Society certified appraiser. She loves the odd and quirky side of historical textiles and is presently involved in several research projects. She is currently exploring the reflection of her Christian faith in her work. Lori and her husband live in southwest Missouri and she homeschools their son.

Lisa Ellis
Fairfax, Virginia
www.ellisquilts.com

Lisa is an artist who specializes in art quilts of spiritual themes that express her faith. She is also passionate about healing quilts and is involved in a number of projects for healing- related exhibitions. She lives in Fairfax, Virginia, with husband and three children.

Barb Garrett
Coventryville, Pennsylvania

Barb is a former high school math teacher who loves the challenge of working with small pieces. She currently does volunteer work with the Lancaster Quilt and Textile Museum and Mennonite Central Committee at their Morgantown ReUzit Shoppe (thrift store) and Ephrata Quilt Room. Barb and her husband have two married daughters and one granddaughter.

Paula Golden
Backsburg, Virginia
www.paulagolden.com

Paula has been teaching quilting for over twenty years and was selected as 2001 Teacher of the Year by *The Professional Quilter Magazine.* She is a co-author of *Quilts of Virginia.* As an enthusiastic fiber artist, her passion for quilting encourages students to explore their own creativity in a positive, nurturing environment.

   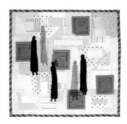 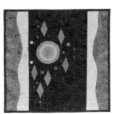 

Judy Gula
Annandale, Virginia
www.ArtisticArtifacts.com

Judy became a spinner, weaver, and dyer in her early teens and later transitioned into mixed media fiber arts including jewelry, art quilts, and clothing. She is a member of Potomac Fiber Gallery in Alexandria, Virginia; and is the owner of Artistic Artifacts, a creative teaching center and supplier of mixed media paper, fiber, and ephemera. Judy lives in northern Virginia with her husband and son.

Mary Kerr
Woodbridge, Virginia
www.MaryWKerr.com

Mary is a long-time quilter who specializes in vintage with a contemporary twist. She currently lectures and conducts workshops that focus on quilt history and antique textiles. She is an American Quilters' Society certified appraiser and active in numerous quilting organizations. She and her husband have three children.

Kathy Lincoln
Burke, Virginia
www.kathylincoln.com

Kathy has been sewing since the age of nine, and teaching quilting since 1992. She has a special passion for simplifying techniques and is always looking for new ways to improve. She and her husband have three children.

Kathy Metelica
Tega Cay, South Carolina

Kathy has been involved in quilting and collecting antique quilts and fabrics for over 20 years. She serves on the board of directors for the American Quilt Study Group and is an active member of the Alliance for American Quilts and the York County Quilt Guild in South Carolina. She has just recently relocated to Grafton, Vermont, as a Retail Execution Manager with the Kimberly-Clark Corporation.

Jane Miller
Woodbridge, Virginia

Jane grew up around quilts but didn't become interested in making quilts until she reached her midlife crisis (Jane thinks this was about age 42!) and realized she needed to do, "...something just for *me*." She had always stayed busy being a mom and working as a public school Speech Pathologist. Now the local quilt guild has opened a whole new world of friends and quilting possibilities. She and her husband live outside Washington, D.C.

Jeannie Roulet Minchak
Moorestown, New Jersey

Jeannie is a quilt artist and designer, specializing in commemorative, heirloom, memorial, and t-shirt quilts, as well as customized designs. Her work has been featured in several magazines and books, and she created organic quilts for AVEDA's Pure Privilege program. Jeannie currently lives in Moorestown, New Jersey, with her husband and tons of fabric waiting patiently for her attention.

  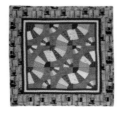   

Jeannette Muir
Medford, New Jersey

Jeannette was a National Quilting Association judge, teacher, and author. Today she is happily retired living at Medford Leas Retirement Community, with her husband. They have two daughters, a son, and six adult grandchildren. During the summer months she has a passion for baseball, especially the 2008 World Champion Phillies.

    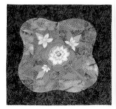 

Sue Reich
Washington Depot, Connecticut
www.suereichquilts.com

Sue began quiltmaking as a child while spending summers at her grandmother's farm in Crawford County, Pennsylvania. As a young mother living in Ohio, most of her quilts were made for the beds of her three young children. Sue is the author of four quilt history books and continues to work as an emergency room nurse. As she contemplates retirement years, Sue says she looks forward to turning her passions —quiltmaking and quilt history research—into her next profession.

Shannon Shirley
Woodbridge, Virginia
www.onceinarabbitmoon.com

Shannon has been quilting since 1989 and started out by focusing on traditional quilt methods. In the past few years, she has experimented with various techniques and especially enjoys the challenge of working on art quilts. Shannon has a classroom in her home and loves the excitement her students bring to each workshop. She is the proud mother of three girls.

Cyndi Souder
Annandale, Virginia
www.MoonlightingQuilts.com

Starting with doll clothes and progressing to award-winning contemporary art quilts, Cyndi has always had the drive to design, sew, and create. She was taught to sew and quilt by her sister, Vicki, and continues the tradition by teaching others. She lives in northern Virginia with her husband.

   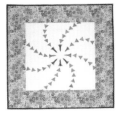  

Pam Weeks
Durham, New Hampshire
www.PamWeeksQuilts.com

Pam is a quilter and fiber artist who has been a state-juried member of the League of New Hampshire Craftsmen since 1993. She has exhibited her quilts nationally and internationally. She was the executive director of ABC Quilts and is an American Quilters' Society appraiser. Her current historical research continues on signature quilts, quilt-as-you-go, and potholder quilts. Pam lives Durham, New Hampshire, in the summer, and in an RV somewhere in the west in the winter. She is the proud mom of one son.

Epilogue

*T*here are not words to express how very much I appreciate the gift of this group's time and talent. Each of these ladies has given without question and freely offered immeasurable support and encouragement. They tolerated my detail-oriented nature and did not blink when they were told their quilts would not come home for a number of years. I am thrilled to share the fruits of their labor as we continue to travel with this exhibit. Who knows in what they will be asked to participate next?

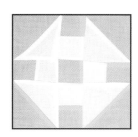

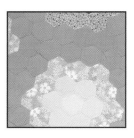

Detail of Mary's Quilt Show by Linda Cooper

Index

Detail of The Friends in Mary's Garden
by Jeannie Roulet Minchak